The surprising, amusing, and often touching
story of what happens when an unconventional
nun crusades on behalf of a bunch of upper
middle-class kids who seem to have everything.

the NEW CHILDREN

by SISTER GUS

Whitaker House
504 LAUREL DRIVE, MONROEVILLE, PA 15146

Copyright © 1975 by Whitaker House
Printed in United States of America
ISBN number 0-88368-058-0

Published by:
Whitaker House
504 Laurel Drive
Monroeville, Pa. 15146

*Some of the names in this book have been changed to protect
the individuals involved. The events are absolutely as described.*

Excerpts from *The Jerusalem Bible*, copyright © 1966 by
Darton, Longman, and Todd, Ltd. and Doubleday and Company, Inc. Used by permission of the publisher.

Contents

Foreword

Based on the life experiences of young people today, this book unfolds with a flow of newness and freshness as they searched to discover God within them.

Sister Gus, as she is called, proclaims to all the Gospel that is ever new and life changing. As she dialogues with and about today's youth, the culminating effect brings home once again the message: the Spirit of God is moving in power across our land to bring meaning and joy into the lives of the alienated youth of today.

This alienation, brought about by pressures from society, parents, and peers, clearly brings to the fore the need that this "lonely crowd" has for a deeper meaning to life found only in Christ Jesus.

The New Children, a book filled with hope and courage, clearly and succinctly relates what one person filled with the fire of the Spirit can do in a world wounded yet crying out to be healed. Many youth in the Cincinnati area can attest to that one person who stepped into their lives with the Spirit of Jesus. We discover them here as they become "New Children."

Michael Scanlan, T.O.R.

Michael Scanlan is the president of The College of Steubenville, Steubenville, Ohio, and author of The Power in Penance *and* Inner Healing.

Preface

Any book concerned with delicate matters of personal counseling and events that touch the very core of our young people's lives presents a twin dilemma. On one hand I want to tell the whole truth because it illustrates so forcefully God's power and love operative in our midst. On the other, I have a serious obligation to protect the confidence and reputation of those to whom I have ministered.

I have solved this problem in the best way I knew: when relating an incident that might cause embarrassment or repercussions, I have changed names and occasionally external circumstances that might allow identification.

In every other respect, these events are recounted as I have experienced them. This is not fiction. It is an account of what I myself have experienced in working with youth who are on fire for Jesus.

In my work in youth ministry in Cincinnati, Ohio, I am daily confronted with the Lord's power at work among the young. I marvel at their openness and zeal. The Lord has put it upon my heart to tell the world what He is doing in the midst of these young people. And He has confirmed it with a Scripture passage from Habakkuk 2:2-3 in *The Jerusalem Bible.*

Then Yahweh answered and said,
'Write the vision down,
inscribe it on tablets
to be easily read,
since this vision is for its own time only:
eager for its own fulfilment, it does not deceive;
if it comes slowly, wait,
for come it will, without fail.'

Sister Gus
528 Rugh Street
South Greensburg, Pa. 15601

1. Memory Bank

"You're out of your mind to attempt such a thing," Bart boomed over the sound of the motor. "They'll have you under investigation before you even get it off the ground." The flinty eyes of Bart Newcomb had a way of underlining his point.

Bart had been "big brother" to me since my Navy Nurse Corps days when he rescued me from an Officers' Club Happy Hour that had gotten a bit too happy. Forty-ish, brusque, aggressive, he was a man of few words, words that were frank and often unpolished. After his Navy tour, he'd gone into real estate. Bart was a shrewd businessman but his marriage of twenty years was a shambles.

This wasn't the first time Bart and I had driven through a park in all its autumn glory. Not too many years before, we were in the same situation and he'd blurted out the same phrase, "You're out of your mind—" Then he was referring to my announcement that I was resigning my commission in the U. S. Navy Nurse Corps to enter the convent of the Glenmary Home Mission Sisters in Cincinnati, Ohio as a member of that community.

"You're giving up your Lieutenant Commander flight nurse status to take orders from some Mother Superior?" Bart asked incredulously. "You're out of your cotton-picking mind!"

In his quieter moments, Bart gave me two weeks until I'd be leaving the nunnery before going wild. Now, thirteen years later, we were riding through another park and I was sharing with him my latest aspiration as a Glenmary Sister—to help develop a youth ministry in Cincinnati. We were to meet his daughter Carla and her roommate for a picnic in the park.

On such a day you've really got to scrunch through autumn leaves in order to absorb all their beauty fully. Bart and I got out of the car and walked toward a group of children playing Frisbee. Bart was pensive, about to explode verbally.

"Who roped you into this deal, Gus? Somebody give you some sweet talk about helping kids get off dope and sex—sort of a crusade?"

Patience isn't one of my strong points. But I tried to be calm in replying as a Frisbee disc went sailing over my head.

"Bart, nobody talked me into reaching out to the kids. I've wanted to do it for years. And I've finally found someone with the same interest who has begun such a work. I want to join him. Like NOW."

"What do you know about this person, Gus? He might be some fanatic, some do-gooder who'll get you all fired up and then leave you in the dust. What background does he have?"

"Now you're sounding like a personnel manager. The initiator of this Catholic youth ministry is Father Richard. He's sent out an appeal for like-minded Christians to join him in the work. I'm interested."

A huge black crow had parked himself squarely in our path and was yakking excitedly to another crow hovering on an overhanging branch. The sound of the crow's call was similar to Bart's staccato questions ringing in my ears. Neither was about to be silent.

12

"Gus, be reasonable," Bart suggested. "What young priest is ever going to convince the hierarchy in the Catholic church that today's kids are in trouble and need something different from the usual catechism classes?"

"Bart Newcomb, you're implying we're defeated before we begin," I commented. "We've been reasonable long enough, sitting back while our Catholic kids leave the church in droves and really get in difficulties—deep ones. Now it's time to step out in faith with all the boldness we can and let the Lord do the rest. And He will! The Protestant churches found that out a long time ago."

"Look, Gus, you asked for my advice, remember? I haven't been inside a church of any kind for years. But I watch them operate. By the time you and this young priest take your plans for the kids through the chain of command, you'll be knocked flat. The way I see it, the top brass doesn't want anybody to stir the waters. It's too predictable in that rut they've been in for a couple of centuries now. I get the feeling some would have been more content if Pope John hadn't opened those windows!"

"I know there are some in the church who are running scared about anything new and different. We've got to take that chance. We've got to be willing to take a few risks for the kids. To be pushed around and misunderstood. If our plan gets vetoed, we'll start over—from another angle. Again and again if necessary. There has to be someone somewhere in the church who will listen and give us the green light. I am convinced that Jesus will raise up leaders in the church who will respond to the desperate needs of the kids. He *will* prepare the way for our work."

I was momentarily stunned as a Frisbee disc slammed into the side of my head, knocking off my sunglasses. Bart salvaged my glasses from among the leaves and

13

after he leveled a verbal blast at the children playing Frisbee, we started back to the car.

"I suspect Carla and Daisy aren't going to get here with that picnic lunch, Gus. Carla mentioned they both had exams this morning."

"We can plan it for another day," I agreed.

"Want to have a quick bite at some nearby restaurant?"

"Thanks, no, Bart. Let's wait until the girls can make it. I'm anxious to hear about their classes this semester."

"Just drop me off at the office then, please," Bart said. "Maybe I can clear some of that mountain of work off my desk since we're not having the picnic."

As we got in the car, the Frisbee players waved to us. The beauty and innocence of children!

"Gus, you know what I've been thinking these past few minutes?"

"What's on your mind?"

"I've been thinking that you sound like a hopped-up Jesus freak!"

"Maybe I am, Bart," I smiled as the ignition kicked over. "Maybe I am."

2. Launch Pad

Me a Jesus freak? Now that was a novel idea! That's what Bart had called me yesterday, and he had been serious. But how could anyone over thirty in this day and age be categorized as a Jesus freak?

The title itself had conjured up a definite image in my mind whenever anyone had used the phrase in the past. To me it had meant one who was young and not too clean: a hippie type who was bizarre in behavior, attire, and decorum, Fundamentalist, not too well grounded in the Scriptures, mainly looking for kicks and companionship. I'd talked with some of them on Fountain Square: a sterile kind of conversation that didn't get too involved or too deep. They seemed sincere; too sincere. Fanatical almost. Yet, though I didn't personally approve of their open confrontation of every passerby with the blunt "Where are you with Jesus?" question, I liked these kids.

My first encounter with a Jesus freak was a liberal education: for him and for me. I was walking briskly across Fountain Square before my parking meter had time to run out, when a bedraggled teen-ager stepped in front of me. He was bedraggled according to my standards, but I have come to learn since that in his own estimation, his attire was proper, comfortable, and practical. He was wearing a pair of Marine fatigues that

15

hadn't seen an iron in many days. The name "Dillinger" was stenciled across the pocket in bold black letters. I thought he was some smart aleck until he smiled and I was completely disarmed. That was only the beginning.

Along with the smile came the soft-spoken remark, "Jesus loves you."

Never in my life had anyone ever said that to me in broad daylight in a city square. And he meant it! I know my facial expression and my reluctance to stay put while he talked gave me away. I tried to step around him, but it didn't work. Dillinger wasn't about to let me go that easily.

"Sister, you look as though no one ever told you that before," my young friend observed.

In my own mind at that moment I was fighting a battle. "After being in the convent for thirteen years, of course I know Jesus loves me," I thought. "Who does this know-it-all think he is to question that?"

Aloud I replied, "I know Jesus loves me. I'm just not accustomed to having a perfect stranger come up to me and initiate a conversation with that remark. Now, I really must get back to my car. The parking meter will run out and I don't want to go home with a ticket. I'm sure you understand."

There! I'd made my pat little speech and I'd soon be rid of this lad!

But Dillinger, the irrepressible, continued, "The Lord will take care of that parking meter, Sister. I'd like to talk with you. It will only take a minute."

Only that morning at our community Mass we had listened to the age-old Gospel from Matthew 25:35-40. "When were You in prison, Lord, and I visited You? When were You hungry and I fed You? When were You lonely and I stopped on Fountain Square to talk with You?????" I couldn't move.

16

Dillinger noticed my hesitation and said, ever so gently, "Why don't we sit on one of the benches here for a minute, Sister? You're probably tired."

I found myself moving inexorably toward one of the benches. What a pair we must have made! I'm definitely a nunny-looking nun and my friend was strictly the hippie breed. But so gallant. With a great flourish, he wiped off the bench before we sat down.

I couldn't take my eyes off his face. He glowed. Not the kind of glow you see when they're high on drugs or booze. An indescribable, other-worldly kind of glow. I kept thinking, "This must be what it's like to be hypnotized. You can't take your eyes off the hypnotist." But I wasn't being hypnotized. I was perfectly alert and aware of my surroundings, queer as they were for this sort of encounter.

"Dillinger, do you always walk right up to people and address them as you did me?" I asked.

"Let's not be so formal, Sister. All my friends call me 'Wreck'."

"Wreck?"

"I guess it *is* a funny name," Wreck laughed at my surprise. "But, honestly, Sister, it's the right one for me. That's what I was before Jesus took over my life, a wreck! He pulled me out of the gutter and He keeps me out and I want to tell everybody about Him. So every time somebody calls me 'Wreck' I'm reminded once more of how much Jesus has done for me."

"How unusual. I have no doubt Jesus has done all this for you but I wonder why you'd want to be reminded of your past every time someone says your name. Don't you want to forget it?"

"No way, Sister. No way. My past has helped make me what I am for good or bad. And like I said, it reminds me of what Jesus has done for me. I give Him the glory.

17

I didn't do it. If it were up to me, I'd most likely still be sleeping with that doll back on Vine Street and getting my fix every day. Do you read me?"

"Yes, Wreck, I understand what you're saying, but it will take me a while to get accustomed to a name like that."

"I know you're busy, Sister, so I'll get on with it. I was sitting here reading my Bible when I saw you come across the Square and the Lord put it upon my heart to give you a message."

"Now this!" I thought. "He hears voices, too. But so did Joan of Arc." Though my mind was blocking everything Wreck was trying to tell me, there was some indefinable something in me that seemed to be saying, "Listen." Now *I* was hearing voices! "I am tired," I told myself. "I've got to get away from this lad and get home."

To Wreck, I commented, "Tell me what you mean when you say the Lord put it on your heart to give me a message."

With an effortless patience, Wreck explained, "I guess that way of saying it may sound different to you Catholics. It means that the Lord let me know He wanted me to speak to you. It isn't like I heard a voice or anything. You know, it's like a very strong conviction inside of you. There's no questioning it. Once you walk with the Lord you just *know* when He wants you to do something."

"I see," I said weakly. But I didn't see at all. Why should the Lord speak to me through this stranger?

Wreck continued. "When the Lord put it on my heart to speak to you, Sister, I didn't want to do it."

"What's the matter? Were you frightened by a nun? I thought you Jesus people would approach *anyone* to tell them about Jesus."

"That's true. We do. But we're still human, and

18

sometimes, we get scared. I was scared because it felt stupid to think of walking up to a nun and talking to her. I never talked to a nun before. Not ever."

"Well now you know we're harmless, Wreck. We get scared, too. So why don't you give me the Lord's message?"

If it were possible, I do believe Wreck's face glowed ever so much brighter as he started to speak. "The Lord wants me to say to you that He loves you and He has a special work for you to do, one that you've never done before. Don't be afraid, Sister. It is His work and He will guide you, even though a lot of people will give you a bunch of static and get uptight. Trust Him."

I couldn't speak. Everything in me was rebelling at what I was hearing and the manner in which I was hearing it. I had experienced prophecy before, but it had always been in the context of a charismatic prayer meeting. Never anything like this during a chance encounter. Chance encounter? Nothing happens by chance when it is the Lord's work. His timing is perfect. I know that from my own life.

Trying to appear composed, I said, "Thank you, Wreck. Pray with me about this. Now I really must be going."

"Sure, Sister. Hey, why don't you come pray with us? We have a prayer meeting every Tuesday night at 7:30. We'd be glad for you to come. Bring your sisters, too, if they'd want to come. Do you know where the Jesus people live?"

"I've never been there, but the house has been pointed out to me. Thank you for the invitation, Wreck. Perhaps the Lord will arrange for me to pray with you all some Tuesday night."

As I darted back to the car, I had the strongest feeling that yes, I should pray with these young people. I had

19

heard that some of our Catholic kids went to their prayer meetings. Why not a Catholic sister? Especially since I had been invited.

The next Tuesday I was there. The impulse to go had become so strong I couldn't deny it any longer. High on a hill overlooking the night lights of Cincinnati, I had my first session of real Jesus-people prayer. This wasn't fun and games for these kids. This was serious, holy business.

I was warmly welcomed and no one seemed to mind that I was the only over-thirty person present. As the evening progressed, the music gained in volume and enthusiasm. I was surprised to note so many periods of quiet prayer when those assembled seemed to be truly waiting on the Lord. In my over-thirty convent mentality, I hadn't expected this element at a Jesus-people prayer meeting. Oh, my, but I had a lot to learn! During one of the intervals of silent prayer, I reflected again on Wreck's "message" for me. Then it nudged my mind. A special work for me to do? Of course. Youth ministry. I'd been praying about that for a long time. I thought of Bart Newcomb and all his objections, objections that seemed to diminish in that moment as I resolved, "Tonight, definitely, I'm sending in my application to Father Richard!"

Following the prayer meeting we regrouped for refreshments. I was walking toward Wreck when another young man intercepted me. He hadn't been too vocal during the prayer meeting but he had appeared to be praying.

"Digger is my name," the freckle-faced lad offered as he extended his hand.

I returned the handshake as I said, "Hi, Digger. I'm Sister Gus."

"Yeah, Wreck told me about you. I made him a bet.

I bet him you must be a Lutheran or Episcopalian nun. He says you're Catholic. Are you?"

"Sorry you'll have to lose your bet, Digger. I am Catholic. Have been all my life since the cradle."

"You can't be," Digger protested. "I've gone to Catholic school since first grade and I never heard a nun pray like you do. You can't be Catholic."

"Do you think all nuns pray exactly the same way, Digger?"

"Every nun I ever heard pray out loud did it the same way. You can predict what they're going to say and the tone of voice they'll use. Always the same."

"Well, Digger, you just keep your ears alert and I think you might hear a different kind of prayer from some nuns and priests these days. We have a great deal to learn from our Protestant brethren in the matter of spontaneous prayer."

"But how come you do it different?" Digger persisted.

"I grew up in an all-Protestant neighborhood. We were the only Catholic family. My folks didn't mind if my brother and I went to church with our playmates so long as we kept our own church obligations. So I listened to the prayers in the Protestant churches and in the homes of my friends, and now it just comes naturally to pray in this way with you here. Or in any other prayer group. Wasn't the Lord good to have prepared me in my childhood for this very night?"

"Wow," was Digger's enthusiastic comment. "What a Jesus!"

"What a Jesus, indeed," I echoed. And I meant it with every cell in me.

Cincinnati is quite lovely at night with her myriad lights and wide parkways. It was late as I drove home and there wasn't much traffic. Mentally I was composing my letter of application to Father Richard to work with him

21

in the teen-age retreat program he was launching for the new school year. The very name was intriguing: TEC—Teens Encounter Christ. Such mystery and wonder and awe those words stirred in me—"encounter Christ"! Anyone who did could never be the same again.

"You've got a lot of nerve, Old Shoe," I mused to myself. "Here you are applying for work in youth ministry and you don't even have a college degree. Everybody has a college degree these days. How can you possibly qualify?"

It's true. I have no degree. I graduated from a three-year nurses' training program. And though I've taken a vast assortment of courses in the Navy and in the convent, they don't total up to enough of the right credits for a degree. The only qualification I can really claim is intense desire. Plus enthusiasm and conviction. You won't find those in any curriculum. There seemed only one solution: apply and let Father Richard decide.

My application went off in the morning mail. Because other activities captured my interest, I didn't think of it again until two days later when I was driving to the post office to pick up our mail. I stopped for a traffic light at Blue Rock and Hamilton and noticed that the man in the car in front of me was waving his right arm with thumb and forefinger meeting. It was the Navy signal for 4.0—right on target! Then I recognized the man. It was Father Richard. He was signaling that he had received my application and was accepting me as a co-worker. The light changed, and he drove across Hamilton as I turned left. "Oh, Lord," I said aloud to no human ear. "I'm so glad. I'm so glad."

When I got back to the convent from the post office, I was called to the phone. Bart Newcomb's foggy voice greeted me. "Gus, I'm coming over to Mount Airy this morning to see a client. Will you be home? I'd like to stop in."

I was surprised to hear Bart so early in the morning. Anything before high noon is the middle of the night to him. "Something important must be on his mind," I conceded to myself as I replied, "Do come, Bart. I'll be home all day."

Bart Newcomb did everything with gusto—even ringing door bells. There was no mistaking who was ringing the bell as the echo reverberated through the convent. I opened the door to a Bart I hadn't seen in two years—not since the day his marriage of twenty years to Marcia fell apart. He was obviously distressed, so distressed he didn't even make his habitual slurs about contaminating the inner sanctum of the nunnery by his presence.

"Has she called you, Gus?" Bart asked.

"Has who called?"

"Carla, my daughter. Has she been in touch with you?"

"Bart, it's not usual for Carla to call me during the week when she has classes. What's wrong?"

"I wish I knew what was wrong." Bart seemed totally frustrated. "I've run my legs off trying to track her down."

"How about her boyfriend Jake? Has she been with him?"

"He's the joker who called me and asked if I'd seen Carla. He says they had a date last night and Carla didn't show up."

"Did you call her sorority house?"

"Yes, but none of the gals there had seen her in days."

"Did you ask your wife Marcia if she's been in touch with Carla?"

"Marcia wouldn't talk to me. Guess that could be my fault, though. I asked her if she thought Carla might be in trouble—like pregnant—and she yells into the phone,

23

'Of course she couldn't be pregnant. I got her a prescription for the Pill so she'd be safe.' And, BAM, goes the receiver in my ear."

"Do you think Carla is on drugs?"

"I don't know. Jake, her boyfriend, always smells to me like someone who's on the stuff. I'll pulverize that guy if he's got her on the stuff, too."

"Did she ever take off before?"

"Once. Right after Marcia and I split up and she found out I was living with someone else. She went to her grandmother's in Indiana that time."

"Bart, did you do something to disappoint Carla again that might drive her away?"

The room was uncommonly silent as I waited for Bart to answer. Slowly, in obvious anguish, the words came. "I'm living with a girl. Carla and Jake bumped into us as we were coming out of her apartment building one night last week. Gus, I'll never forget the look on Carla's face."

Again the silence punctuated only by the chiming of the grandfather clock in the hallway. Bart was bent in half, weighed down by his humanity. He didn't seem to have enough ginger to move.

Looking at his agonizing form I prayed to the Father Who loves us all, "Father in heaven, lift this terrible burden from my friend. Keep his daughter safe and help us find her. Somehow let Carla know that she is loved. We love her but You loved her first. Guide her back to us. We ask it in the all powerful name of Your Son, Jesus. We thank You for hearing our prayer and—"

My prayer was interrupted by my call bell. I picked up the phone and a young woman's voice spoke. "Sister Gus, this is Daisy. I'm Carla Newcomb's roommate." (I hoped she didn't hear my intake of breath.)

"Is Carla all right?" I asked.

24

"Carla's sick. Bad. That's why I'm calling you. I didn't know where to get help. And she doesn't want her dad to know. Promise you won't tell him?"

"I think you had best tell me the whole story before I make any promises."

"Well, Carla took some stuff Jake gave her and she's real sick. She won't go to the hospital because they ask all kinds of quesions and she doesn't want to get Jake in trouble. See?"

"Yes, I understand. Where can I meet you?" I asked.

As Daisy gave me the address on Calhoun Street, I shuddered. Past experiences on Calhoun Street had been wild, but there was no time to be a cringing female now. "Lord, be with us," I prayed.

I dashed back to the front room, putting my coat on en route, and was about to tell Bart about the call just as he raised his head and said very soberly, "In the past few minutes, Gus, I think I realized for the first time why you'd want to get involved in this youth ministry stuff. The kids really are hurting. My Carla, too."

"Grab your coat, Bart. We can talk about it on the way. Let's go find Carla and tell her that she's loved!"

3. Programming the Spirit

Carla Newcomb had a tight squeak. Some tall praying, some dogged nursing skill, some tender loving care pulled her through the worst of the storm.

Seeing her writhing on the bed in a smelly, ancient apartment on Calhoun Street, I wondered why anyone would take the stuff when they always run the risk of a bad trip. Undoubtedly Carla took it because she hoped it would bring her freedom and love. Instead it brought her pain and misery and desolation. Had she learned a lesson? And had her father, Bart?

Throughout the whole episode, Bart charged about like a caged animal. At one point he went out searching for Jake. Fortunately he didn't find him during the peak of his fury.

Carla's girlfriend Daisy and I took turns sitting with Carla. When she was over the bad trip, Daisy and I packed her and a few essentials into Bart's car. He was taking Carla to her grandmother's in Indiana to rest and gain back her strength. She had about as much zip as a wet noodle. I had the impression that Carla wasn't all that grateful that we had saved her from self-destruction. I ached deep inside for all the Carlas of the world.

With Carla still very much in my awareness, I left Calhoun Street behind and headed for the Franciscan monastery in Mount Airy. Father Richard had scheduled a meeting of the team members who would be working on the first girls' TEC of the new school year. We were to review the retreat agenda and pray together.

The night air was nippy with a hint of frost as I pulled up in front of the monastery, an old building rich in history and tradition. The whole team seemed to converge on the monastery parlor at the same time. Quite an assortment: a mother of two teen-agers, a mother of four under twelve years of age, a registered nurse, a student nurse, a high school senior, Brother Tony, Father Richard, and myself.

In his presentation of the retreat agenda and goals, Father Richard mentioned that the TEC retreats would have a different thrust this year compared to those of past years. The retreat would not be a hand-holding, gee-it's-great-to-be-here kind of retreat. The retreatants wouldn't be fed pablum. They would be fed on the real meat of the Gospel. Already I was becoming excited, but one look around the monastery parlor told me that not everyone present shared my excitement. There were pinched faces, hands clasped tightly, bodies rigidly erect, fingers strumming on the end table.

Father Richard reminded us that we would be dealing with needy kids—not needy in the poverty-stricken sense of that word, but needy in a much more tragic sense. These kids were in need of love, in need of trust, in need of compassion, in need of understanding. Some of them had been crushed by overpowering family problems. One had tried to take her life. One was pregnant. All of them came from upper middle-class families, so money was no problem. They had everything, materially speaking. Everything but love. They had to snatch love wherever and however they could, no matter how fleeting the encounter. Inner rage boiled in many of them. The kids

27

were restless, seeking, struggling to find a meaning for their life, yearning to belong.

At this point, I hurt so much inside I wanted to bawl. Typical female! But that was the whole reason I was here: to try to help ease the hurt in the kids' lives a little, to proclaim to them that, "Yes, somebody *does* care about you and that somebody is me. And the main reason I can care about you is that Jesus loved you first!"

Father Richard continued his briefing. "We have deliberately kept the retreat as unstructured as possible. This isn't meant to be comparable to a classroom situation with which they have to live in school. We want the retreats to be swinging, open, with radical commitment burning at the center. And this, my friends, presupposes that we deal quite honestly with the quality of our own life in Jesus."

I noted a swift glance between the student nurse and the high school senior at this moment. The mother of the teen-agers looked alarmed. There was a definite shifting of papers and sitting positions. The registered nurse remained aloof, but perhaps that was due to her being among strangers. I was wedged snugly in my corner of the sofa and for some goofy reason, I was humming a funeral dirge to myself—the *Dies Irae* that we formerly sang at funeral Masses. How strange!

Even before we began to pray together, I realized that the team didn't gel. There was a breach in our fortress somewhere. The funeral dirge was prophetic. Our prayer together should have been an inner journey for the whole team, coalescing us into a vibrant body with Jesus in the center, a body of people who were liberated and fully available to those we would be serving in the next three days. Instead, some were obviously threatened by the whole situation. I don't think it was from a feeling of inadequacy. There seemed to be a deeper reason for their discomfort. From my own experience, I know that you cannot address yourself in prayer to Jesus as Lord unless you know Jesus as a person. Several in the monastery parlor didn't know Jesus as a person. It was too late now to make changes in the team. Somehow we would have to learn that we needed each other and would have to support each other "where we were at."

The inner journey which should have been the central common discipline of the team members ground to an uncomfortable halt as we prepared to leave. Some seemed in an uncommon rush to get out the front door. I lingered behind to talk with Father Richard for a few moments.

"Where, oh where, did you collect these gems?" I asked referring to the team.

"This is one situation I hope to correct in time," Father Richard answered. "I can't make too many changes right at the beginning. The high school senior and student nurse are former TEC-ites so they feel competent to be team members. But the TEC they made last year isn't anything like the one coming up. The other women are friends of priests here in the monastery and wanted to do something to help the kids. They have very good intentions. But we both know that good intentions aren't what these kids *really* need."

"Sounds to me like you'll have as many problems with team members trying to get their own heads together as you will with the kids," I said, my enthusiasm diminishing.

"Very possible. But we have some other things going for us. Some of the brothers here at the monastery will be fasting the whole three days for us. The people at St. Pat's charismatic prayer group will be praying for us. So go home and get a good night's sleep," Richard advised.

"A good night's sleep?" I roared. "I'm going back to the convent chapel and have an all-night prayer vigil!"

"Great," Richard called as I walked toward the car. "I just might do the same here."

I was serious about the prayer vigil. Our convent chapel is in a separate building from the convent, so it is possible to be there at any time of the day or night without disturbing anyone else.

In the dim, warm chapel, it would have been so easy to be lulled asleep by the silence. Shuffling through the dry leaves searching for some juicy tidbit, our cat made the only sound in the night. I was too distressed to be sleepy. Gnawing at my brain was the realization that the team members I had left a short time ago were on much varied wave lengths. Plus the fact that some very important elements seemed to be missing: a love and knowledge of the Scriptures; a personal relationship with Jesus; a prayer life; a commitment to serve the kids on retreat. It didn't seem unreasonable to me to expect this sort of life style of our team members. These should be the marks of every Christian.

"Jesus," I prayed, "such a mess. How can we make any progress this way? You can't give what you haven't got. I don't understand how we can lead these forty girls to You if some of our team members don't even know You. Maybe I'm being harsh, Jesus, to growl about this so vigorously. Help us, Jesus. Send your Holy Spirit to scorch us where we most need to be scorched. Each one of us, Jesus."

Somewhere off in the night an owl hooted its mournful cry. I shivered involuntarily. Then I found myself saying out loud to no one but the chapel walls, "Now it's ridiculous to get in such an uproar. No doubt the Lord has planted us together as a team for a very specific reason. Who knows what I may learn from the other team members? For each of us, this is a first-run amateurish

30

affair and we will all end up helping one another. Amen to that!"

I prayed for a teaching from Scripture and opened my Bible. The words danced off the page from 2 Corinthians 12:9, *"My grace is enough for you."* Those few words said it all. No further need to fret. I would simply lift the whole thing up to the Lord in prayer, summon His Holy Spirit, reach out to the team members and retreatants so that they might be touched and healed deep within by the love of Jesus. Was it possible that I heard a bird sing just then? At this hour of the night? But it wasn't night any more. The chapel clock registered 5:30 A.M. A new day!

When I arrived at the TEC Lodge later in the day, some of the team members had already arrived. I had been singing the song "I Will Raise Him Up" all day—couldn't get it out of my head. It seemed a singularly appropriate theme song for the three days coming up. As I looked around the TEC office at the other team members gathered in a circle, I saw them in a new light. "Thank You, Jesus, for the graces of the night just past," I prayed. There was a last-minute review of the agenda and Father Richard led us in prayer.

It happened then. As we were concluding those halting, hope-filled moments of prayer, there was a thunderous banging on the TEC office door. Our first carload of retreatants had arrived. We were in business. What a welcome we gave them!

The influx of girls, baggage, and parents kept us busy until we had everyone settled. Preliminaries, ground rules, and general information were dispensed methodically. Then came the "Trust Walk." We were each paired off with someone we didn't know, one blindfolded, the other to act as guide. Out into the frosty night we went. In the first two minutes of the Trust Walk I landed flat on my

31

posterior. The parking lot was icy. After that my partner was overly solicitous, which gave me a clue to her beautiful gift of compassion. When we finished the Trust Walk and were coming together as a group to discuss our reaction to the experience, I said to my partner, Rachel, "I'm going to write your mother a note and tell her what a kind and gentle daughter she has."

"Don't bother," Rachel muttered.

"Why on earth not, Rachel?" I asked.

"She probably wouldn't be able to read it anyway," Rachel commented.

"Rachel, I'm so sorry. I didn't know your mother was blind."

"She isn't blind, Sister. It's just that she's drunk most of the time."

A feeble "Oh, I see," was all I could muster at that moment. "Jesus," I inwardly cried, "bless this beautiful child. Let her realize that You love her. We love her. She is precious."

Rachel moved off to sit with several of the girls from her school. I sat beside one of the girls whom I hadn't had the opportunity to greet as yet.

"Hi, I'm Sister Gus," I said to a very well-dressed young woman. Her clothes indicated she was definitely upper, upper middle-class. I had noticed when she arrived that she came alone in a Volvo.

"Hi," a soft voice said. No more. She deliberately looked away from me. I noticed that her name tag said "Chrissie." Well, I'd have three days to try to break down that frigid barrier!

It was a circus trying to get the girls to bed. They couldn't unwind. Most of the team members decided to go downstairs and try to get some sleep. I elected to stay upstairs in the dormitory. I have slept in so many different barracks in my Navy Nurse career that I didn't anticipate any difficulty sleeping in the midst of the melee. Pillows zoomed around me. Girls high-stepped over me. But I held my pad! Ensconced on my mattress on the floor, I was ready for sleep.

Sleep wasn't to come that easily. I'm sure the girls thought I was asleep. When we had our survival courses in the Navy, they had taught us how to lie perfectly still so that you appeared literally lifeless to anyone passing by. And I just used that little technique in this instance.

I heard one of the girls on a nearby mattress whisper, "Are you ready for me to get it out now?" I thought she was referring to a bottle. Although alcoholic beverages were prohibited, my acute olfactory nerves told me that someone in that room was drinking wine at this very moment.

"Yeah, why don't you?" another voice answered. I expected to hear the sound of tinkling glasses and a gurgling of liquid. But what I heard was the sound of something flat being moved and set in place.

Another voice asked, "What is that thing?"

To which the first voice replied, "Hey, stupid, haven't you ever seen a Ouija board before?"

"A what?"

"A Ouija board. It's groovy. Answers all your questions. Just ask it a question. Go ahead, just ask it," the agressive one prodded.

I had the strongest inclination to rise up from my mattress and smash that Ouija board. The work of Satan right in our midst! How cunning of him to introduce such a trap for young, inquisitive minds. Anything to keep them away from finding the only real true answer—Jesus!

"Jesus," I prayed, "Whatever is evil here in this room I command You to take authority over it. In Your all-powerful name, Jesus, I ask You to bind the forces of evil here present. I ask this in Your name, Jesus, and I thank You for hearing my prayer."

33

At precisely that instant, from some corner of the room, a basketball came pummeling right in the center of the Ouija board. Suddenly the girls seemed more interested in getting revenge against the girl who had thrown the basketball and the action moved off to a far corner of TEC Lodge.

"Thank You, Jesus. I hope that devilish board is knocked out of commission forever," I thought as I rolled over in the hope of catching a few winks before morning.

As the retreat progressed and the team gathered together before each conference for prayer, I had hoped to see some sign that the general attitude of the team was improving. I guess I'm like the apostles in Matthew 12:38 when they said, "Master, we should like to see a sign from you." If anything, they seemed more withdrawn. The retreatants were a potpourri of untapped energy. Some in their sophistication scoffed at everything that was said and everything that was done. Several had stayed up all night and dozed through the day's conferences. Hidden beneath the veneer of sophistication, though, I knew there were deep wounds. Real torment.

During the retreat I gave my testimony of how Jesus had taken over my life after years of carousing around as a Navy flight nurse and years of a ho-hum convent existence. Following the conference Priscilla, an apple-cheeked red-head, cornered me and asked, "Sister, do you have to go through *all* of that to find Jesus?"

"Oh my, no," I replied in all honesty. "Priscilla, you can find Jesus right now, right this very moment, by just asking Him to take over your life. He's such a gentleman, Priscilla. He's never pushy. You have to *ask* Him to come into your heart."

With the lovely candor of a simple child, Priscilla said, "But I don't know how."

34

"Then I'll help you, Priscilla," I said, full of hope for this radiant young woman.

"First off, make sure you have forgiven all those who may have wronged you in any way. Tell the Lord in your heart that you do forgive them."

Priscilla was silent for a time. "Funny that you should say that," she commented. "Earlier today when Father Richard was talking about reconciliation I thought of this girl, Olivia. She thinks she's so high class. Real sexy doll. I can't stand her because she took my boyfriend away from me. Is that what Father Richard meant and what you mean—that I have to forgive her for doing that? She's sneaky."

"Olivia sounds like a girl who needs our prayer very much, don't you think, Priscilla? Girls who try to be real sexy, as you say, are usually very lonely. And though she may have attracted your boyfriend away from you for a time, she probably doesn't have any real friends."

"Gee, I never thought of it like that, Sister. I guess I do forgive her, since she probably isn't responsible for trying so hard to win all the attention," Priscilla said with all the wisdom of one advanced in years.

"Now, Priscilla, whatever you have in your heart that may be keeping you from the Lord, just ask Him to bind it and lift it from you—things like astrology, ESP, Ouija boards, fortune-telling. You have to renounce them and push them out of your life, Priscilla."

"Heck, Sister, that's not hard," beamed Priscilla. "I never did fall for all that jazz anyway. I don't think anyone can predict the future unless that person gets a sign from God some way. But that's too complicated for me to worry about. I take each day as it comes."

I looked into the shining blue eyes of Priscilla and was overwhelmed by a great love for such simplicity and the Lord Who gave her such a gift. I continued, "Priscilla,

35

in your heart or aloud, whatever way you prefer, say this prayer with me."

Priscilla had her head bowed and her hands, palms upward, resting on her lap. She was surely praying as I began to say the words softly, "Jesus, I praise You and thank You because You are Lord. I ask You to forgive me for the times I have failed to live Your Gospel. Come into my heart, Jesus, right now, and take over my life. I want to live only for You. Thank You, Jesus."

Two big tears rolled down Priscilla's face and plopped in her lap. Then, with the quickness of a gazelle, Priscilla had enfolded me in a bone-crunching hug and was squealing, "Sister, Sister, Jesus is so real. He's so real!"

The bell for the next conference drowned out the remainder of Priscilla's jubilation. I was ready to do some squealing myself. During the next conference, it was my turn to go to the chapel to pray. I was glad for the time to be with the Lord to thank Him for Priscilla and her many gifts and to ask His special blessings and graces for the remainder of the retreat.

All afternoon on the last day, the girls planned the climax of the retreat, the communion celebration at 5:30 P.M. They made all the decorations, planned the music and readings, set up the altar and furnishings. TEC Lodge was buzzing with activity. Shortly before 5:30 TEC Lodge started to fill with people, since any boy, girl or team member from a previous TEC could return for the closing liturgy. Tears flowed in copious quantities about midpoint in the liturgy, when the girls realized the community they had formed in the past three days was about to be disbanded. The Kiss of Peace was unrelieved chaos. It was glorious. Until I got to Chrissie. I looked into two dark eyes that held more misery than any I had ever seen before in a seventeen year old. For the Lord's own reasons, I was prompted to say to her, "Chrissie, whatever the burden is on your heart, I pray that Jesus will remove it."

Chrissie glared back at me and barked out the words, "Do you believe all that crap?"

Very sincerely I replied, "Yes, I do believe it."

"Well, Sister, you're wasting your time," Chrissie snorted as she pulled my arms from around her neck.

That was too much for my Yugoslav temper. "O.K., Chrissie," I blazed. "It's my time, see? And if I want to waste it praying for you that's precisely what I intend to do. Understand?"

"Hell," she fumed and turned on her heel and left the altar.

I was a wreck. "I really goofed that one," I thought. And I was convinced that I had goofed badly when everyone but Chrissie came to the altar to receive the Body and Blood of our Lord. In the general bedlam that followed the liturgy as the kids were all saying their farewells, Chrissie said goodbye to everyone—everyone but me. "Jesus," I prayed, "lift the burden from Chrissie. Give her Your love and peace. She's Your baby, Lord. Do it. Now." The last part of my prayer was swallowed up in the sound of the motor of Chrissie's Volvo as she revved it up and sped off into the darkness alone.

Crammed into the past three days had been an array of emotions from sheer frustration to great joy, from discouragement to hope, from tears to laughter. These girls had touched my life deeply. In what state would Rachel find her mother when she got home tonight? Drunk again? Priscilla had nearly floated out the front door of TEC Lodge. The eyes of Chrissie, filled with misery and pain, haunted me.

Several days after the retreat, Father Richard called. "Some of the kids want to have a prayer meeting tonight at 7:30 here at the monastery. Can you come?"

"Oh, yes, Richard, I'll be there," I bubbled as I waltzed away from the phone. Just what we had been hoping for — a follow-up for the retreats. How nice that the kids initiated it themselves. It would mean so much more to them. "The next step will surely be a Scripture class. It's inevitable," I thought, reconsidering my own past experience. The deeper you get into prayer, the hungrier you are for the Word of God. And vice versa.

We gathered in the monastery parlor: four guys, three gals from the last TEC, three Franciscan brothers, Father Richard and I. Significant that there should be twelve of us for the first prayer meeting. A fat, green candle was lit in the center of the room and Joe Weiss's "Lord, Teach Us to Pray" was playing in the background.

Our prayer was hesitant, low-key to begin. Momentum seemed to be building as we continued to praise the Lord. We sang the simple melody, "Spirit of the Living God," rather softly. And then all glory broke loose. As the words of the song say it so well, "Fall afresh on us." That's what the Spirit did. One by one, those of the young people present who had not yet received the baptism of the Holy Spirit received the infilling. Some quietly; some audibly; some tearfully; but all joyfully. Quite spontaneously we broke into "Amazing Grace" and nearly blew the rafters off the monastery. There's no programming the Holy Spirit. None of us could ever have predicted that our first follow-up prayer meeting for the TEC retreats would generate so much fire and power.

In a moment of quiet, Sam spoke. "Can you imagine what this next boys' TEC is going to be like?" he asked. "Five of us here are on that team. Wow!"

"Let's start now to fast and pray for those young men who will come to us," advised Father Richard. "The Holy Spirit is moving, and I have a feeling there is no slowing Him down. Praise Jesus!"

4. Cool It

There were twenty of them before me. I counted them. Twenty different sitting positions. True, you would need the elasticity of a teen-ager to be able to assume some of those positions. As I looked over this group of lads on my first boys' TEC, I hadn't yet realized how unique each young man would be in behavior, reaction, personality. And sprawl!

Before the boys started to pile into the TEC Lodge, the team gathered for prayer. We were a diverse conglomeration. The jocks on this retreat would be able to identify with Sam who was a football and basketball letterman in high school. Now a college soph, he'd dropped the sports. Bo was quiet but deep. A natural-born ham, Cullen oozed Ireland. Brother Tony was still trying to find himself.

Father Richard echoed my own prayer as he began, "Father, we praise You and thank You for the trust You place in us to guide these kids so that they may know Your Son as a real person in their lives. We are poor instruments. We have no claim to great gifts or great talents. Use us to accomplish Your purpose. We place ourselves and all these kids in Your hands. Praise Jesus!"

As we, the TEC team, sat in our prayer circle in the small TEC office, I thought of a football huddle. But we weren't calling any signals. Jesus was doing that. Before the game even began, we had one sure promise that no football team can ever claim before a game: we knew that our team would win!

Ending our prayer on an upbeat of praise to the Father, we rose to leave the office and face the Twenty. Cullen, his usually ruddy face rather pale, tapped my shoulder and whispered, "Hey, Sister Gus, I don't think I want to go out there. I've never done this before. I'm scared."

"That makes two of us, Cullen." I tried to convey a confidence I didn't have at the moment. "Just hang in there, man. My woman's intuition tells me we're about to launch off on a great adventure like nothing we've ever experienced before!"

Sam, who looked like an All-American champ from the front cover of *Sports Illustrated* magazine, towered over my mere sixty-one inches. He leaned down to my size and said confidentially, "Some of these guys must have stopped at the tavern at the bottom of the hill before coming here. Smell that booze?"

"Yes, I noticed the aroma when the lads were registering. But we've got to take them where they're at. For some of these guys maybe that's the kind of fortification they needed to give them enough courage to walk through the door to begin this retreat. It can be scary for some," I acknowledged as I focused on one pimply-faced lad who was vigorously chewing the last speck of flavor out of his gum. "Jesus, be with us," I prayed. We walked toward the Twenty.

School cliques were deliberately broken as the boys were divided into groupings of four with a team member at each table. Ground rules were given and a few getting-to-know-you techniques applied before the real meat of the retreat began.

For the next three days the Twenty would travel from darkness through the shadows into the light. This was

40

not meant to be a people trip, a sitting-around-in-a-circle, isn't-it-great-to-be-together kind of group dynamics. Jesus would be the center. Hopefully the lads would reach the point where they would take the leap of faith and want to turn their life over to Jesus. It wouldn't be easy. It would be rough for all of us.

I had gone outdoors to escape the cigarette smoke for a while at the break time. Brother Tony evidently had the same need for fresh air as he joined me. "Say, Gus, are the guys at your table any more with it than mine?"

"They haven't found a spot to plug in yet. Can't rush it."

"I think these guys are more interested in resuming their poker game than they are in the retreat."

"Give them time, Tony. Give them time to unwind."

"I don't think we're getting through to them, Gus. They look so bored with their I'm-here-because-I've-got-to-be-here kind of look."

"Don't let that facade fool you," I cautioned. "These kids are like every other teen-ager these days. They're hurting. And we're here to help them find the answer— Jesus. So let's get with it!"

As Brother Tony and I turned to re-enter the building, I noticed someone standing in the shadows. At first when I saw the flared pants and windbreaker, I thought the person was a man. As my eyes became accustomed to the darkness, I noticed the silhouette—definitely female.

"Do you know her, Brother Tony?"

"I saw her hanging around here earlier in the evening. Maybe she goes with one of the guys on retreat."

The monastery bells were chiming midnight when I commented to Brother Tony, "Something tells me I'd better check."

I walked toward the shadows and looked into the face

41

of a teen-age girl. Her eyes were hard and cold, like steel. Her gaze was fixed on me as I greeted her.

"Hi. I'm Sister Gus. What's your name?"

"Mimi," she answered briskly.

Her windbreaker was open and I could see that her sweater was a size too small. One of the women-libbers, no doubt. The night wind was rearranging her long, bleached hair. Her steely eyes stared at me.

"Are you looking for one of the guys on retreat, Mimi?"

"None of your damn business!" She spit the words at me.

With effort, I tried to keep my tone even. "I think you'd best move on, Mimi. These lads are here for retreat and that's serious business."

That remark touched a nerve. The steel in her eyes was white hot as she snarled at me, "You damn nuns are so stupid. How would *you* know what those guys need?"

I looked intently at Mimi. Without knowing why or how the words came, I heard myself saying, "Mimi, what these lads need is Jesus Christ. And so do you!"

Then it happened. Totally unprepared, I didn't think to raise my arm to ward off the blow that came. Mimi let me have it, hard, right in the mouth. I could feel the blood oozing inside my mouth as my teeth bit into my lip. Still too stunned to realize the full impact of the past few moments, I couldn't see too well as Mimi whirled away from me and dashed across the parking lot. I think she was crying.

With a grinding of gears and screeching of rubber Mimi ripped out of the parking lot in her car. I tried to formulate a quick prayer for her as she careened off into the night. Slowly I made my way back into the building, hoping my face didn't mirror the last few minutes too accurately.

By now some of the lads were back into their poker game. Others were gabbing. A few had gone to bed. I made my way to the bedroom alcove downstairs where I'd be sleeping. Something deep inside me was hurting for all the Mimis of the world this night who had no one to tell them they were loved. No one to reach out to touch them in their utter loneliness. I knew deep in my bones that some other time, some other place, I'd see Mimi again.

Many sleepy eyes greeted me in the morning. "Will they never learn?" I thought. "You can't play poker all night long and expect to be bright-eyed in the morning." The stereo was blaring away many decibels too loud. Everyone seemed to be disjointed. The whole morning was like that.

Father Richard summoned the team for a conference and we decided to give the retreatants a block of time after lunch so they could catch a few hours' sleep. The team would spend the time in prayer. Some of the brothers at the friary were fasting these three days for the retreatants. With that kind of powerhouse behind us, some good would have to come from these days. Father Richard would be spending the afternoon time giving a workshop on faith at a local school, an assignment he hadn't been able to reschedule outside retreat time.

An overpowering lethargy seemed to have settled over the team as we came together for prayer before resuming the retreat. "These guys don't seem to be with us," Bo observed.

"The poker game is their crowning achievement," commented Brother Tony. "I wonder what would happen if we hid the cards."

"I feel like I've made one big goof after another. I got into an argument with one of these dudes about

43

Transcendental Meditation. Man, I don't even know how to spell it, much less define it," Sam moaned.

"Be glad they're talking about meditation, any kind of meditation. The jokers at my table are planning to get out their joss sticks. Next thing they'll be breaking into their incantations," Cullen observed.

"Don't give up so soon. Some of these lads are doing a bit of dying," I said. In the back of my mind was the vision of Mimi dashing across the parking lot into the night. I wondered if any of these lads was her man.

"Let's lift them all to the Lord in prayer," began Father Richard. "This retreat is in His hands. Let's just praise the Lord and thank Him for what He's going to do in these young men tonight. We claim His promise that anything we ask in His name will be granted. I'm hoarse from all the talking I've had to do at the workshop this afternoon. Drained. I don't feel like I've got anything more to give. You do it, Jesus. Thank You, Jesus."

A basketball thudded against the office wall. So many shouts and sounds swirled around us. "I need you, baby; oh, how I need you," groaned from the stereo and pounded in my head. "Oh, Jesus," I prayed, "do You hear us midst all this uproar? We love them, Jesus. Help us bring them to You."

After some time of silent prayer, Bo spoke. "I asked the Lord for a Scripture teaching for us and I'd like to share with you what He's given me. It's from the *Good News for Modern Man* translation, 2 Corinthians 12:10: *"For when I am weak, then I am strong."*

"Thank You, Jesus, for Your teaching," Richard prayed.

"Right on, Jesus!" Cullen exclaimed.

Bo seemed relieved as he said, "Looks like we're all in the same fix. I thought I was the only one feeling lost and useless."

44

"I still think we should hide the cards," Brother Tony muttered.

Fortified with the word of the Lord and His promise that He would be strong in us, we called the retreatants together and proceeded to the point of the retreat where we would consider reconciliation and forgiveness. Admittedly these aren't the world's most popular topics. Father Richard, in a husky voice, captured their attention as he repeated with varied nuances: *"You are loved.* No matter what you have done or where you have been, you are loved. Jesus loves you." The age-old message. Ever ancient, ever new. The very hoarseness of his voice seemed to lure the lads into listening more intently.

Each person listening was invited to write down what he found most displeasing about himself and bring the paper to the chapel. The group was quiet, meditative it seemed, as they wrote and as they walked to chapel. Such a contrast from only an hour before.

The monastery chapel was dark except for one light which accentuated its monastic atmosphere. In a charcoal brazier before the altar, a fire was burning. I read them the story of the Prodigal Son from Luke 15:11-32. Brother Mark played and sang, "And the Father Waited." Indeed, He was waiting: waiting for each of the lads there. Waiting quietly, patiently, lovingly.

Slowly the lads circled round the fire and threw the slips of paper on which they'd written into the flames. With "Amazing Grace" playing in the background, Father Richard said, "As these flames consume your faults and hangups that you have thrown into the fire, so Jesus' love consumes you. My brothers, I proclaim to you the Good News that you are forgiven and Jesus loves you."

As the flames diminished, I looked around the group and saw an astonishing sight. Tears were streaming down some of the faces. Some were embracing each other.

Several had gone to the altar steps and were kneeling in prayer. The atmosphere was electric.

Father Richard had left the sanctuary and invited any who wished to receive the sacrament of reconciliation to come individually into a room off the chapel. The rest of us on the team stayed in the chapel to pray and watched a glorious drama unfold before us—one that was absolutely unexpected, unplanned but never to be forgotten. Even to the most inexperienced eye it was apparent that the Holy Spirit was at work. His presence was so real it was palpable.

It would have to be the power of the Spirit to bring such a change in an all-star jock now kneeling by the altar with tears running down his cheeks. Not weakness. Not slush. Only the pure unadulterated joy of the Lord that comes to a young man when he throws off all the earthly garbage and takes on Jesus as the Master of his life.

Sam squatted on the floor beside me. He had just exchanged a rib-cracking bear hug with one of the retreatants. "Gus," he whispered, "something is happening here. This place is alive!"

"Jesus is doing it! When we are weak, He *is* strong—if we just get out of the way and let Him do it," I replied.

Several of the lads were singing very softly. "Amazing Grace" never sounded lovelier. Though there was a feeling of subdued dynamite, it was quiet—a peaceful kind of quiet that comes of silence pregnant with prayer.

A do-it-yourself pizza party had been scheduled following the reconciliation service. But no one was moving. All the lads seemed to be oblivious of time, perfectly content to remain at prayer. Their facial expressions were calm and peaceful—even the pimply-faced lad who was always wildly chewing a wad of gum. The peace and

46

calm that comes from the inside. The peace and calm that comes with knowing the Lord Jesus.

I was bursting to share the wonder with Richard but he was still hearing confessions. "Jesus, how You spoil us if we just put everything in Your hands. Thank You!"

Brother Tony was restless. On his way out of the chapel, he leaned toward me and grumbled, "These guys are a bunch of freaks. A bunch of kooky freaks!"

Before I could comment, he stalked out of the chapel. "What a strange reaction," I thought. "I should think he'd be overjoyed to see these lads wanting to turn over their lives to Jesus." At that moment of grace, no one could have predicted the repercussions that would result from this night.

For various reasons, none of us slept much the night of November 7, 1971. The following day, the last day of the retreat, seemed a foretaste of Gloryland. Everybody was in high gear, happy and bubbly, really joyful. All except Brother Tony, who appeared sullen and uncomfortable. The lads planned their own closing liturgy. Surely the roof was raised several inches in our enthusiasm, yet there were also moments of quiet prayer. This was truly a celebration.

In the general chaos of final farewells as the Twenty were departing, Father Richard was called to the phone. Some time later he returned and his facial expression indicated troublesome news. Not until the last retreatant had gone did he reveal how troublesome.

Very soberly Richard said, "The Top Brass want to see me. Tuesday I must appear before the TEC Board. They want to know what kind of wild things we did on this retreat. They accused me of using psychological manipulation on the kids."

"I've heard the Holy Spirit called by many names but never a psychological manipulator!" I commented.

47

Sam caught the last part of my sentence as he prepared to leave. "Who's a manipulator?"

"The Holy Spirit," I said.

"He is?" grinned Sam. "Wow, what a way to go!"

Father Richard looked utterly exhausted. No doubt he had died more than any of us these three days.

"Richard, are you too weary to pray together before I leave?" I asked.

"I'd like to. I need to."

We were both weary, a wonderful kind of weary. The TEC Lodge was suddenly so empty and silent. Our prayer was halting and short, a prayer of gratitude to our Father Who loves us, a prayer of praise for the lavish gifts of God's love that we had shared in these days. The end of our prayer was punctuated by the door slamming as Brother Tony went out into the night without a word. Perhaps it was a premonition, but as I watched him go off into the darkness I had only one thought in my mind—Judas walking toward the High Priests.

5. The Burden of Restlessness

"I'll give it to you straight without any flourishes, Sister," the urologist began. "If we're to give you and that left kidney of yours a few more years, we have to do renal surgery now."

With that perfunctory announcement, my urologist was gone. Providentially, I didn't have time to probe him with endless questions. Nurses know too much about health matters for their own peace of mind anyway when they're on the *receiving* end. I was a typical nurse-patient: curious, questioning, restless.

Countless objections bombarded my brain. "I can't afford to take time out now." "Surely there must be another solution rather than surgery." "The TEC program is just getting started; I might miss something important." Lurking on the periphery of my mind was the somber possibility that the surgery wouldn't be effective and I'd be shuttled to that damnable dialysis machine.

"Whoa, Old Shoe," I mused. "You can't squander any more time on mental gymnastics. Unsheath your most powerful weapon—Jesus—and give it all to Him!"

"Peace be with you," is a phrase I've said a zillion times in our Catholic liturgies. On this day it had a sparkling new meaning and I was uplifted by the peace of Jesus surging through me. Uninvited, the tears rolled down my face—tears of tranquil joy and serenity that

49

can come only from deep-down peace. It was in this damp condition that Father Richard, Brother Dennis, and some of the kids found me when they came to visit. There was snow outside but it was springtime to see them. They were open and genuine and unabashedly Christian. I needed them and they knew it.

Quickly I briefed them on the urologist's ultimatum. Without flicking an eyelid, bony and elongated Mitch droned, "Why don't we have a prayer meeting? Right here in this hospital room. Now."

Magically my blah hospital room was transformed into a jubilant arena of prayer and praise. Brother Dennis felt moved to pray for a healing for me, but in my heart I knew this wasn't the kind of witness the Lord was asking of me at this time. Intuitively I knew that I would have the surgery but I didn't cringe when I thought of it now. It was as though I had swallowed some pungent elixir that erased the fear. In truth, I had. The elixir was the power of the Spirit Who replaces fear with peace. Refreshed by the prayer, supported by the body ministry, I was ready to submit to surgery.

The pre-operative whirl and anesthesia are a great blur in my memory. I had a sampling of several post-operative complications and my hospitalization was prolonged. During this time, Father Richard was scheduled to appear before what I dubbed "The Inquisition"—a board of his peers who would determine what was right and what was wrong (in their opinion) with the TEC program in general and the last boys' TEC in particular. Never in my life have I felt so utterly trapped. I wanted so very much to appear before that board, too, to give them a non-Franciscan point of view of what transpired on that boys' TEC. Appear before the board? What a joke! I couldn't even get out of bed. The Lord really has His ways of showing us that He'll do the job in His way and in His time.

Frantically I flailed my pillow. I wanted desperately to be able to speak in behalf of Father Richard and the whole TEC program including the follow-up prayer meetings. Why was I so fretful? The Scriptures say it so well: if it is the work of the Lord, it will flourish. And this youth ministry was the work of the Lord so no inquisition could blot it out. Since Father Richard's family name is Rohr, I have referred to him often as Richard-the-Lion-Hearted. In my frustration, I envisioned Richard as a lion gobbling up the members of the inquisition board. Oh, wouldn't that be a tasty mouthful! Though I couldn't get out of the bed, there was no obstacle to my praying. In prayer I asked for a Scripture teaching and opened my *Good News For Modern Man* to Revelation 5:5. "Don't cry. The Lion from Judah's tribe has won the victory." The Lion? Richard? Surely. I wept.

Jabbing at my mind was the sudden awareness that I wasn't alone in my room. Hesitantly I opened my eyes to see a bundled figure standing at the foot of my bed. Could it be? Yes, underneath the parka it was Chrissie! She shifted her position nervously and twirled the ends of her long hair around her fingers. I was wishing she were close enough so I could give her a big bear hug.

"Jesus," I prayed, "Don't let me goof again with this young lady. Give me the right words so that I may say what she needs to hear."

Banishing the image of our last encounter from my mind, I smiled a greeting. Chrissie's eyes were soft and bright now. Something definitely had happened in the life of this child of God. Something wonderful.

With those limpid eyes looking right at me, Chrissie said very softly, "I just came to say thanks." As quickly and quietly as she had entered my room, she was gone.

Oh, the wonder and power of Jesus' love. When we ask Him for a miracle, He gives it to us! The remarkable change in this young woman in so short a time was surely a miracle. I don't know what happened in her life to change her so completely. I don't have to know. Jesus knows and that is quite enough.

The jangling of my phone jarred me out of my reverie. Father Richard's voice sounded bone-weary as he informed me that his session with the inquisition was completed.

"Don't keep me in suspense, Richard. What did they decide?"

"We can continue the TEC retreats with no mention of the Holy Spirit and no more prayer meetings at the monastery," Richard replied without expression.

"So who needs to mention the Holy Spirit? He'll do all right without any sales build-up from us! At least we can continue with the retreats, Richard. That leaves only one problem: where to have the prayer meetings."

"Brother Dennis has a lead on that, Gus. The Lord is with us. I'm sure."

"So am I, Richard. And just to confirm it, when you have a moment tonight read Revelation 5:5."

"Is that another one of your famous Scripture teachings?"

"Read it and see if it isn't right on. It's not mine; it's the Lord's."

"I will, Gus. Rest well. See you tomorrow," Richard's voice was almost a whisper as he hung up. He'd most likely been talking a great part of the day, not wanting to blunder or overemphasize or water down his strong convictions. Father Richard had enough of Christ in him to waken the comfortable conservatives from their lethargy. Jesus never did promise that Christianity would be fun and games! As one of the kids had written on my get-well card: "May the peace of Christ continue to disturb you!"

Dominating my convalescence was the urgency of locating a new place for the prayer meetings. On November 19, 1971, about three dozen young people came to initiate our new location: the only pink house on Brookside Avenue. Brookside Avenue would never be the same again.

Most of the kids preferred to sit on the floor. Because of my recent surgery, it was wiser for me to choose a chair. A young man sat near me and as more continued to come and bodies were rearranged, he was nearer and nearer until he seemed to be sitting on my toes. I have never seen so much hair on one male before. The hair stuck out at all angles as though electrified, plus moustache, plus beard. He was one hairy ball until he turned around and smiled. My hairy friend introduced himself as "Marc, a drop-out."

"A drop-out of what, Marc?" I asked.

"High school first. Then work. Then society in general."

"If you're a drop-out of society, how is it you happen to be here tonight?"

He was bluntly honest when he replied, "I heard some cute chicks come to these wingdings."

I smiled my understanding of Marc's attitude as I thought, "That may be the reason why you came this time, young man, but it won't remain your motive for coming back. Jesus will make a new man out of you if you let Him."

Father Richard greeted everyone in the name of the Lord and asked all newcomers to introduce themselves. The hairy ball at my feet repeated his drop-out history and then commented, "I figured I didn't have anything to lose by coming just once."

53

Brother Dennis began singing "Amazing Grace" and our first prayer meeting in the pink house was off to a magnificent start. These were ordinary bright-and-breezy teen agers sans theological background or degrees. A few giggled in their uncertainty but most were splendidly serious from the very beginning. Most had come because they wanted to know Jesus better. Some, like Marc, were curious. Some were looking for kicks.

All the Scripture readings that night fell into a pattern emphasizing our nearness to the cross of Christ and the need for repentance. My hairy friend asked to borrow my book and I handed him my Bible. He was rustling through it as we sang, "Jesus is Lord."

During the period of silent prayer that followed, Marc pointed to a passage of Scripture. "Look at this, Sister," Marc whispered. "I keep opening to this same quote every time."

"The Lord is trying to tell you something, Marc, and all the rest of us, too. Why don't you read it to the group," I urged.

"Out loud? In front of everybody?"

"We all need to be taught from the Word of God, Marc."

"Hell, Sister Gus, I've never read the Bible before in all my life. I'll mess it up good."

"Just open your mouth and let it come out, Marc. This isn't a contest of reading ability. We're all here to seek the Lord. You can help us."

Hesitatingly, like a small child, the great hulk of hair began to read from the Scriptures, the words ever ancient, ever new from Revelation 3:15-22.

I know all about you: how you are neither cold nor hot. I wish you were one or the other, but since you are neither, but only lukewarm, I will spit you out

54

of my mouth. You say to yourself, 'I am rich, I have made a fortune, and have everything I want', never realising that you are wretchedly and pitiably poor, and blind and naked, too. I warn you, buy from me the gold that has been tested in the fire to make you really rich, and white robes to clothe you and cover your shameful nakedness, and eye ointment to put on your eyes so that you are able to see. *I am the one who reproves and disciplines all those he loves:* so repent in real earnest. Look, I am standing at the door, knocking. If one of you hears me calling and opens the door, I will come in to share his meal, side by side with him. Those who prove victorious I will allow to share my throne, just as I was victorious myself and took my place with my Father on his throne. If anyone has ears to hear, let him listen to what the Spirit is saying.

As Marc neared the end of the reading, his voice was softer but firm as though he were trying to mask his bewilderment. I felt my own pulse quicken as I listened to the Scripture. Quite naturally I reached forward and put my hand on Marc's shoulder. He was trembling. As I prayed silently that the Lord would help Marc be open to the promptings of the Spirit, Father Richard prayed aloud with a gentle persuasiveness:

"Jesus, we praise You and thank You for Your Word. Let our ears be open to what You have to tell us. Don't let us be lukewarm. Continue to fill us with Your lavish love so that we may be on fire with Your zeal for the Father's kingdom. Help us to repent. Remove from our hearts everything that is not of you. We lift up our brother Marc in a special way and ask You to bless him with Your peace and love. Let him know how much we love him because You have loved him first. May Your Spirit come upon him and mold him into a new man, your man. We ask this in Your all-powerful name, Jesus, and we thank You because You have heard our prayer."

Spontaneously, we all began to sing "Spirit of the Living God" as Father Richard vested for the celebration of communion. At the end of the song, the group was quiet except for Marc. He was singing in the Spirit; his voice would soar to high notes rare for an untrained male voice, and then the tone would cascade down. The glow in his eyes was dazzling and his impish smile intrigued me. He's been wearing that same impish grin ever since that November night.

I had intended to stay on the porch of the pink house for only a few minutes to inhale some fresh air and then return indoors for the Mass which was about to begin. As I turned I noticed the doorway was filled with the large frame of Jazz, our guitar player, and he didn't seem inclined to move. Something was eating at him.

"Sister Gus, can I ask you a question?" he muttered.

"Let's sit on the bottom step, Jazz, and we won't disturb the kids inside."

"Sure. Any place is just fine. Want me to get your coat?"

"No, thanks. I'm enjoying the fresh air."

"I just gotta ask somebody, Gus. It's bugging me something fierce."

"What's bugging you, Jazz?"

"That dude in there. The one who was sitting by you. He's bugging me."

"Marc? I didn't think you knew him. This is the first time he's come to a prayer meeting."

"Yeah, I know it is. And you're right; I don't know him. But I just don't understand what he was doing, like there at the end before you came outside."

"He was singing in the Spirit, Jazz. That's one of the

56

gifts of the Holy Spirit you receive when you come into the fullness of the baptism of the Spirit."

"Maybe I'm stupid or something, Sister Gus. I've always gone to Catholic schools and now Xavier University and I just don't dig this baptism of the Spirit that you're telling me about. Savvy?"

"I understand your puzzlement. The Catholic church is waking up to some of the treasures she formerly had in the early Church. Some don't talk about it because they don't understand; some don't speak of it because they mistrust the charismatic movement and figure if they ignore it, it will go away. But it's blossoming and mushrooming all over the world."

A patrol car drove slowly down Brookside Avenue. Seated next to the driver was a stern-faced policeman who peered into all the parked cars. He was about to question us when Jazz gave him a friendly wave and cheerily said, "Praise the Lord!" In a side whisper he said to me, "That'll frost his kidneys. These fuzz are all the same. Every time they see you sitting beside a girl they think you're trying to make out and tell you to move on."

"Even when you're sitting beside a nun?" I asked.

"You're female, aren't you?" Jazz retorted. "Besides it's nighttime and he probably didn't notice your veil."

The patrol car proceeded down the block as I resumed the conversation. "Jazz, do you seriously mean you haven't heard anyone, not even any of the guys on campus, talk about the pentecostal movement?"

"I've heard a few of the guys mention it but I'd never repeat what they said until I had time to clean it up a little."

"You mean they ridiculed the movement?"

"I mean they said it involved a bunch of kooks who believe all this crap about speaking in a queer way that's

57

supposed to be praying and going on an emotional binge with Jesus. Freaked out, man. But without drugs, see?"

"Do you know if these same young men who said these things have ever been to a prayer meeting?"

"Are you off your rocker, Sister Gus? Those birds wouldn't be caught within a mile of anything that has 'prayer' of any kind connected with it. They said the chicks they were dating went to a prayer meeting. And you know how dolls blab."

"Maybe they weren't just blabbing, Jazz. They might have accurately described a type of prayer meeting. There are different kinds. Some are freaky. But they're not in the Spirit. That's why the Spirit gives us the gift of discernment so we can tell the difference."

"Let's consider this prayer meeting tonight, Sister Gus. That's what's at me now. Tell me if I'm wrong. The church tells me I received the Holy Spirit when I was baptized, right? And I received the gifts of the Holy Spirit when I was confirmed, right?"

"Right on both counts."

"So how come now you're giving me the business about the fullness of the Spirit like this is some added attraction?"

"It *is* an added attraction, Jazz, that Jesus in His great love gives us if we are open to receive it. The baptism in the Spirit is a new infilling with the Spirit. It's not magic or voodoo. It's a free gift from a Father Who loves you very much."

"Are you telling me that this guy Marc or anybody like him can sashay into a prayer meeting and all of a sudden be zonked?"

"If his heart is prepared to receive the fullness of the Spirit, yes. And so can you."

"No way, baby. No way. I'm all for the fellowship and

58

I really dig the music or I wouldn't be here. But just don't go praying over me, Sister Gus. Promise?"

I looked into Jazz's somber face and answered, "I promise you, Jazz, that I will never pray for the infilling of the Holy Spirit for you until you ask me to do it."

"Don't hold your breath till I ask! Hey, I didn't mean to keep you out here all this time, Sister Gus. We'd better get inside. I told the kids I'd play that new song we wrote with Father John. 'Tough Love.' You'll like it."

As Jazz and I got up off the steps, the patrol car returned going in the opposite direction this time. "We should invite the fuzz inside, Sister Gus."

"All right. Let's do it," I agreed as we walked across the sidewalk.

The patrol car stopped and the driver rolled down his window. He looked as though he were in his early twenties. He greeted me with a "Good evening, Ma'am," that had a Kentucky twang.

"Officers, we're having a prayer meeting inside and we thought you might like to stop in for a moment," I invited.

The stern-faced one blurted, "You're having a what?"

"A prayer meeting," Jazz added. "Really swinging. You'd enjoy it."

The stern one continued, "A prayer meeting on Brookside Avenue? I've been on this beat for fifteen years, and I never heard of a prayer meeting here except over at St. Pat's church. And that's on Sunday night. Are you stringing me along, lady?"

"No sir, I'm not. Do come see. At least to the door."

To his young companion he grunted, "Keep the motor running, Clinton. I'll only be a minute. I've got to see for myself."

The police officer walked with Jazz and me across the street and up the steps to the pink house. Jazz slowly opened the door and we inched inside. We had come just as they were passing around the cup of wine. The atmosphere was one of quiet and reverence although there were wall-to-wall teen-agers squished together on the floor. Someone started to sing very softly, "I Have Decided to Follow Jesus." The song increased in volume and by the last verse everyone was standing. I had become so enmeshed in the singing I hadn't noticed when the police officer left the room. Jazz gave me the signal that our friend of the night had departed. Too bad he didn't get to hear the concluding hymn, "How Great Thou Art." The rafters were raised a few inches by that one.

Young people were piling out of the pink house. Some were reluctant to rush off but parental rules had made midnight the mandatory time to be home. Father Richard had sent a letter to the parents of each of the young people who had been on TEC to inform their parents of the follow-up prayer meetings and extend an invitation to them to come along. Several had come and I found myself studying their facial expressions during the prayer meeting. Quite a study!

The stocky man walking toward me was probably a parent. He wasn't smiling as he extended his hand and introduced himself as "Tom Quartz, Abby's father."

"Is this the first time you've been to a prayer meeting, Mr. Quartz?"

"Yes, Sister. The first and the last."

"You seem very sure of that, Mr. Quartz."

"This stuff isn't my cup of tea, Sister. No offense meant, you understand. I realize the kids pray differently now than when I was back in my teens. I'm glad I came this once so I'll know what Abby is raving about when she comes home. But once is quite enough for me."

"We're glad you came this once, Mr. Quartz. Abby

60

is very special, and it's a joy to know her father is a man who has enough interest in his daughter to come see where she spends her time. Even though you may not return again, please do keep us in your prayers that we may be the kind of leaders these young people need to lead them in a deeper walk with the Lord."

"I don't know exactly what this 'deeper walk with the Lord' stuff is, Sister, but it brought my Abby out of the gutter and I have to be honest enough to admit that. Like I said, it isn't for me. But I'll clobber anybody who knocks it because I know what you've done for my girl. Thanks, Sister."

Silently I praised the Lord for having granted Mr. Quartz the insight to appreciate what Jesus was doing in Abby's life. So many parents are blinded by their own prejudices and hang-ups and don't allow their children any freedom to search for an individual way of finding Jesus.

Under a Russian Cossack-type fur hat, the graying hair of Mr. Brian Abercrombie poked out in an unruly fashion. He looked like a character from one of Walt Disney's animated cartoons. I had never met Mr. Abercrombie before but I had read his daily column in the newspaper often. It was usually caustic and peppery. I was soon to discover Mr. Abercrombie's personality was much like his written word.

"I'm glad you're able to be with us, Mr. Abercrombie," I began. "Your son, Roger, is a talented young man. Do you think he'll follow your career in journalism?"

"No, I don't think so," Mr. Abercrombie replied in a clipped manner. "Anything that I do or like, he'll not do likewise. It's a matter of principle with him."

"Perhaps it's more coincidence than principle, Mr. Abercrombie. Roger is searching like so many other

61

young people. He may change his mind several times before he settles on a career."

"Listen, Sister, I know my own boy! And I know that mulehead won't go into journalism because I'm in it. It would be the same if I were a doctor or lawyer."

"Do you ever talk to each other?"

"Talk? I've talked myself hoarse trying to get this kid of mine to see he's throwing his life away getting tangled up with these Jesus freaks. I want him to go out for sports. Make a name for himself. But not Roger. He'd rather go to a prayer meeting. Damn stupid kid!"

"Roger isn't stupid. He's an intelligent young man who is capable of very deep thought and follow-through."

"He gets that from me: the intelligence. But I don't know where he gets this streak that makes him want to be some kind of evangelistic nut. How can you be proud of that kind of activity?"

"You should be proud of the fact that he is a young man who can think for himself. And be proud, too, that there is at least a fragment of communication between you so that he could tell you this much. That's so important."

Brother Dennis offered Mr. Abercombie a cup of coffee and a snack at this point in our dialogue. He wolfed it down in a few seconds it seemed. I doubt that he even knew what he had eaten. His mind seemed to be drenched with suspicion and mistrust.

"You're like all the rest of the nuns I've ever met," Mr. Abercrombie exploded. "You've never had any kids of your own but you go around telling everybody else how to raise theirs!"

"I don't have to have borne children of my own to reach out to them in trust and understanding, Mr. Abercrombie. Nor do I need to have been married to a man in order to be able to understand what's troubling him.

"And what do you think is troubling me?" he asked.

"I sense in you a feeling that you have failed in bringing up your son because Roger hasn't followed in your footsteps career-wise and in the sports world. I see you as a man capable of giving much love to your family and afraid to do it because you feel it might make them think you're a softie. That's what I see."

Silence. Deafening, uncomfortable silence. Mr. Abercrombie stared at the coffee grounds in the bottom of his cup. The others in the room sensed that we ought not to be interrupted.

I knew my voice was trembling but I felt I should continue. "Mr. Abercrombie, don't be afraid to let your family see how much you love them. That won't make you appear weak in their eyes. It will help them know you as the great man you have the potential to be. I take comfort in the fact that you are here tonight, whatever your motive for coming. Your presence here shows me you really do care about Roger, no matter how much you fret about him."

Brian Abercrombie never looked up at me. He plunked his coffee cup down on the nearest table, muttered a "Good night" and stomped out of the pink house.

I quickly glanced around the room to spot Father Richard so that I might tell him about Roger's father in case there was any feedback. Brian Abercrombie's pen was powerful and nothing was sacred as far as his column was concerned. An energized bundle of red slack suit stopped me from moving further.

"Oh, Sister Gus," she gushed. "I've wanted to meet you for so long. My Edie has told me about you so often."

"I'm glad to know you, Mrs. O'Dell. It's nice that you came to share our prayer meeting and liturgy."

"Oh, I wouldn't have missed it, Sister. Not ever. To

see all these young people so alive and praying. Now who would ever have thought we'd live to see the day that young people would want to pray?" And she giggled.

It seemed so incongruous for a fortyish woman to be giggling. Nothing about her was still. She flitted from one chair to another. I so wished I could harness her in one spot long enough to talk sensibly with her.

"Oh, Sister, isn't that Father Richard a living doll? Such a young priest, too. And so-o-o-o-o holy!"

"He is young, Mrs. O'Dell. But he'd be the first to object to your holier-than-thou image of him. One of the reasons he can communicate so well with the young is that he's himself. As soon as they think any of us are putting up a facade, they turn us off. I think your Edie would agree to that."

Now she was whispering as though we were involved in some foreign intrigue. "Tell me confidentially, Sister, don't you find it hard to be working with such a nice young priest? I mean—with your vows and all."

"Mrs. O'Dell, my vow of celibacy doesn't require that I work with only old, ugly priests. My vow doesn't stop me from being a woman. If it did, I'd end up a shriveled prune. And there are plenty of shriveled prunes in the world without my adding to the number!"

"Oh, you are so clever, Sister Gus. I just never did understand why you girls don't get married but I guess that's your choice."

"It is a choice. And I have willingly made it to be able to serve the Lord more fully in the way to which I feel He has called me." I was losing my patience with this meteor. Streaking from one subject to another, there was no predicting what item she would choose next.

Mercifully, she started to put her coat on. "Oh, Sister Gus, I'm so glad I came. I'm delighted my Edie comes, too. Now you be a good girl," she warned, shaking her forefinger at me as though I were a small child.

"Goodnight, Mrs. O'Dell. We're pleased you came." I saw her to the door and was grateful for the fresh air as she bounced down the steps.

"Who was she, Gus?" Richard asked. "I never did get around to greeting her."

"Edie's mother, Mrs. O'Dell. She thinks you're a living doll."

Father Richard groaned. "Another one who wants to mother me, no doubt."

"Seriously, Richard. I'm grateful you sent that letter inviting the parents to these follow-up prayer meetings. That should eliminate some of the wild speculation about what really goes on here, and we might convert a few of them in the process."

"It has the makings of a separate apostolate in itself —to work with the parents. I just want to tell the whole world what Jesus has to give them. If they are only open to receive it."

The police siren shrilled down Hamilton Avenue only a block away. I wondered if it were our two friends from earlier in the evening who were answering someone's call of distress. In my heart I prayed that their target wasn't one of our kids speeding off home to beat his parents' curfew.

6. The Night People

Arctic blasts, ice and sleet, nothing seemed to deter the kids from coming to the prayer meetings. The numbers increased and the pink house was bulging on Friday night. We praised the Lord for our dilemma and began to search for a new meeting place. Of those offered, the choice made was Our Lady of the Angels High School where we enjoyed the hospitality of the Oldenburg Franciscan Sisters for some months.

There was no predicting what incident might take place during the prayer meeting while we were all occupied indoors. Several car batteries were stolen, usually on the coldest, blusteriest nights. The screeching of tires and gears of cars racing around the school parking lot punctuated our prayer. Occasionally there would be a rumor that some group intended to disrupt the prayer meeting by coming in drunk. So as a matter of policy, before each prayer meeting, we lifted the whole evening up to the Lord. If the meeting were to be disrupted, somehow it would be in His plan.

Bart Newcomb had been promising for months to "look in on your Jesus freaks." With Christmas and New Year holidays past, he surprised me one Friday by calling and inviting himself to our prayer meeting. I had hoped he would bring Carla along, but the wounds were too deep and hadn't healed.

I picked up Sara Kate and Molly before going down North Bend Road to Bart's apartment. Molly's mother shrieked into the night as we drove off, "Mind you, girl. You be home by eleven tonight. Hear?"

"Just ten more months, seven days, five hours and twenty minutes and I won't have to hear that 'you be home by eleven tonight' ever again," Molly sighed.

"That's only a mother's natural concern," I suggested.

"Natural concern, my foot," Molly answered. "My Mom doesn't trust me. She doesn't really believe I'm going to a prayer meeting."

"Where does she think you're going?"

"To a pot party where there are guys. She thinks if she puts the curfew on I won't have time to shack up with any of them."

"Does your mother think I'd take you to a pot party?"

"Hell, Sister Gus, my mother doesn't trust anybody. She probably thinks you're one of my chums with a scarf on her head. Mom has never looked at you in the eyeballs or she'd know you're for real."

"Have you ever invited her to come along?"

Molly laughed loud and long. "Sister Gus, you are a hoot. My Mom enjoys blowing her stack. If she came to a prayer meeting and saw and heard what was really going on, she wouldn't be able to yell at me any more."

"You should ask her, Molly. She might give you a jolt and come some Friday," I suggested as we stopped in front of Bart's apartment.

Bart was bundled to the earlobes as he strolled out to the car. He still walked like a Navy officer on his way to a dress-blues inspection. As he slid into the front seat, I noticed his face. So weary and empty. I wondered what his bunny girlfriend was doing tonight. After the introductions, I suggested to Bart that he help himself to the chewing gum in the glove compartment.

67

"Chewing gum? What in the hell do I want with chewing gum, Gus?"

"You smell like a distillery. It might help."

"Yeah, guess you're right. I had a few martinis before you came. Figured I needed to be fortified before I face all those Jesus kids tonight."

"Why would you be afraid to face us?" Sara Kate asked from the back seat. "We take you like you are."

Bart was silent after that remark.

As we followed the traffic stream down Colerain Avenue past Mount Airy Forest, I thought of the first time I had met Sara Kate. She had been on one of our girls' TEC retreats because it was a school requirement for every senior to make a retreat. The alternative: no diploma. Sara Kate walked in with that I'm-here-because-I-have-to-be attitude. From the first glance I knew she was from an upper middle-class family. Her clothing told me that much. She had the sophisticated air of so many who attend private academies. No one else from her school was making the retreat so she drifted from one small group to another. No ties anywhere.

Something about Sara Kate's eyes bothered me. When she smiled, her eyes didn't. It was as if someone had pasted that smile on her face and it would crack at any moment.

On the first night of the retreat, I found myself standing beside Sara Kate. None of the other kids or team members were around. Without even knowing why, I looked straight at her and asked, "Sara Kate, where are you with Jesus?"

Sara Kate laughed, an eerie, spooky kind of laugh straight from a Frankenstein movie. But she wasn't putting it on. She meant that laugh. Her eyes seemed to have the devil himself dancing in them as she stared at me and answered my question.

"With Jesus? You're the one who had best get with it, Sister. I don't have anything to do with Jesus. I've been in a witches' coven for the last four years. That's living. Man, have I seen fantastic things happen at those sessions. Wow! But I sure haven't seen anything fantastic happen here on this retreat with your Jesus!"

I could smell the sulphur. The hair on the back of my neck was standing straight up. I felt as though I had inverted goosebumps all over me. Only the Spirit could have been responsible for what happened next because I was too weak in the knees to do it on my own. I looked into the hellish face of this young woman who had such great potential to be lovely, fresh and charming as I replied.

"Sara Kate, you just give Jesus a chance and you'll see fantastic things happen in your life like you never dreamed possible."

Sara Kate snorted—a crude sort of sound like you'd hear from an animal. Without another word, she darted outdoors. At our team meeting, we prayed especially for Sara Kate to be delivered from her tormentor. Some of us decided to fast for the rest of the retreat. I called several Spirit-filled friends greatly committed to body ministry, and they readily agreed to fast and pray for Sara Kate and this retreat.

The next day Sara Kate seemed to be swallowed up in the group. I had asked the Lord to provide the opening so that I could build on our brief conversation of the previous evening. I opened my Scriptures to pray, and there it was staring me in the face: "Some demons are cast out only by prayer and fasting" (Mark 9:29).

A movie was scheduled and the girls had rearranged chairs to get a better view. Sara Kate came in late and the only empty chair was the one next to me. Reluctantly she seated herself and maintained an icy silence throughout the movie.

When the lights came back on, Sara Kate didn't move with the rest of the girls. She glared at me and asked, "Why did you say that to me yesterday?"

For a moment she had me off guard. "Say what to you?"

"That bit about 'where am I with Jesus'?"

"Don't you usually ask a question because you want an answer? I really wanted to know the answer to that question so I asked you."

"Oh." That was all. She moved off quickly toward the powder room.

Some strong conviction way deep-down kept telling me that Sara Kate was special. Each of the girls was special, true. But the Lord seemed to have something extraordinary in store for Sara Kate. I intended to pray about it through the night. An all-night prayer vigil always cleared the atmosphere and got my priorities in the right place.

The prayer vigil was a stormy one. No doubt about it, the devil was going to use every trick and snare to keep Sara Kate with her witches' coven. And he was going to use a few tricks on me that night, too. There were times when all I could do was speak the name of Jesus. A terrible oppression seemed to weigh down on me and I tried to shake it. Ordinarily, I am much at peace when I sit quietly in the monastery chapel. On this night, it was as though I were sitting in the center of a swinging honky-tonk. I prayed for strength and guidance. The Lord seemed to be telling me to stay put. His grace would be sufficient for me.

At dawn I was exhausted. I walked up near the altar and prayed, "Jesus, help me. Show me what to do for Sara Kate to bring her to You. Help me." I sensed a

Presence that gave me great peace and courage. As I walked toward the TEC Lodge a bird was singing. Very unusual for Cincinnati in winter.

At breakfast I didn't see Sara Kate. Since some of the girls never ate breakfast, I didn't think it unusual. I looked for her during the first conference and couldn't find her. Coffee break was a noisy time, and I didn't hear the voice that spoke the first time. As I turned, I saw the speaker was Sara Kate. Perhaps it was because I hadn't been to sleep for a while and my eyes were playing tricks on me; but she looked different. Something had changed in her face. She spoke again, and this time I did hear when she said, "Sister, does knowing Jesus really make any difference?"

I nearly popped inside. I tried to simmer down enough to answer. "Sara Kate, knowing Jesus and letting Him take over your life makes you brand new. All the old garbage is swept away by his lavish love that He gives you because you are so special to Him. You only have to ask Him to come into your heart."

So much more I wanted to say. But it was as though the hand of the Lord were upon me, telling me that for now this was enough.

Sara Kate smiled a weak smile but it wasn't pasted on this time. She walked slowly toward the monastery. It was a free time for the girls and I sensed she was going there to pray. "Jesus," I prayed, "Walk with her. She's so special." At that precise moment, I was stricken with a severe headache and became violently sick—green sick. I dashed for the ladies' room completely dismayed at such a physical manifestation of the devil's power. "But there is a power greater, Satan old boy," I thought. "And I claim it right now—the power in the name of Jesus."

By the time I was collected together again and less

71

green, I made my way to the monastery chapel where the concluding liturgy was about to begin. It was a vibrant, alive kind of communion that the girls had planned themselves. When we got to the Kiss of Peace, I turned to face Sara Kate. I was breathless. Her face glowed with the kind of light that comes from within. All she could say was, "It really does make a difference, Sister Gus. Jesus does make a difference." Then we both sort of melted into a pool of tears.

Now, three months later, Sara Kate was riding with Bart and me to a prayer meeting. She had been very faithful from the very beginning of her commitment to Jesus. Whether her former acquaintances in the witches' coven had tried to lure her back, she never said. But I praised the Lord every time I looked at her, to think of the wonders He had brought about in her young life once she had opened the door.

The parking lot at Our Lady of Angels High School was full. That would mean a large group for the prayer meeting. I inched the Dodge Dart next to a battered Volkswagen. As we walked toward the entrance, lanky Mitch came running up with a jolly "Hi!"

"Sister Gus, I just gotta tell you. This will blow your mind!" Mitch exploded.

"Do tell us, Mitch, before you burst."

"Remember last week when we prayed for Larry's friend?"

"The alcoholic? Yes, I remember."

"Well, after I went home last Friday, that kept bugging me. I couldn't get the guy out of my head and I don't even know him. So I called up Larry on Saturday morning and told him. Would you believe, he'd had the same experience? He couldn't sleep all night thinking about this dude. So we met at St. Francis Seraph church and went to every bar on Vine Street until we found the guy. It wasn't even noon yet and he was pretty well along getting boozed but good. We started filling him with coffee and some chow and he sobered up after a while. Larry and I went back to his room with him, helped him get cleaned up and shaved and then before you know it, we started talking to him about Jesus."

"Praise the Lord," Molly chirped. "We'll really have to praise the Lord tonight to thank Him for bringing you to Larry's friend."

"Hey, not so fast, doll. It wasn't all that easy. Just about the time I thought he was ready to give his life to Jesus, he'd get worried about what his buddies would think. I got the inspiration to ask for a Scripture teaching for Larry's friend and I opened to Hebrews 11:1 that says, "What is faith? It is that which gives substance to our hopes, which convinces us of things we cannot see."

"And it hit me like a bulldozer. Like, wow, man! Not only did Larry's friend need faith that Jesus could change His life. Larry and I needed faith, too, to convict us that we needed only ask and Jesus would do the rest."

"Don't keep us in suspense, Mitch. What happened?" Sara Kate urged. Bart was mute. I wondered if he were even listening.

"Larry and I, without any signals, started to pray in the Spirit. I felt as though something wonderful were happening but I couldn't see anything different. The room, a real dump like you find all along Vine Street, all of a sudden smelled like a pine forest. It was wild, man! Then Larry's friend stands up straight and tall, raises his arms, and starts praising the Lord and crying like a baby—but he's smiling, see, the whole time. Out of sight. Just out of sight. Wow!"

"We do rejoice with you, Mitch," I replied just as excited as he. "Let's go inside and tell the others."

73

As we neared the school building entrance, Bart whispered, "Gus, I think I'll get a cab home. I don't fit into this kind of jazz."

"How do you know you don't fit in until you've experienced a prayer meeting? No two are alike. Perhaps the Spirit will lead this one with your specific needs in mind."

"Are they all turned on like this Mitch character?" Bart asked.

"Bart, it's pretty hard for anyone, young or old, to remain placid when they've witnessed a first-class miracle right before their eyes. How many alcoholics have you known who have been transformed while you watched?"

"It was probably a coincidence."

"Then it's a mighty wonderful coincidence. I choose to accept it as an answer to prayer. Right in the Gospel it tells us that we will see even greater things than Jesus did while He was on earth if we only believe."

We were inside the doors now. Rachel met us and took our coats. I introduced Bart to the kids who were near and we found ourselves an inch of space. Brother Dennis began to play "Amazing Grace" on the piano and the prayer meeting was off to a lively start.

A young man who looked and smelled as though he'd had too many beers before he came into the prayer meeting leaned over and whispered to me, "Hey, Sister, are you going to tell any stories tonight? I wanna hear one of your stories."

"We're not here to tell stories, my friend," I answered. "We're here to praise the Lord."

At that moment, Brother Dennis intoned, "Rejoice in the Lord Always," and everyone stood up. The young man with too many beers wasn't very steady on his feet and I tried directing him toward a chair on the sidelines.

Before I even realized what was happening, Cullen and Sam were on either side of the young man gently leading him toward the nearest exit.

I returned to my place beside Bart and he muttered, "Real classy clientele you've got here, Gus."

"The door is open to everyone, Bart." We were all holding hands and singing the Our Father. Bart was on one side of me and Rachel on the other. Rachel's touch was soft and gentle, like herself. Bart's hand was large and rough. I thought back over twenty years when we held hands then in a Navy Officers' Club across the world in Tokyo, Japan. Oh, the diverse paths we had both traveled since that night!

We were singing the line, "Deliver us from evil," and I realized I was praying for Bart Newcomb, praying that Jesus would change his life. There was so much greatness in this man that could be salvaged. He was dead while yet alive. And that shouldn't be.

Following the song we sat and several of the kids gave their testimony of what the Lord had done in their life the past week—nothing earth-shaking or phenomenal. Just the nitty-gritty of everyday life. They were joyful and lively and so sincere. Bart appeared to be listening. "Holy Spirit, let him hear what he needs to hear this night," was my fervent prayer for Bart.

Rachel leaned over and whispered, "Sister Gus, guess what gift I just prayed for?"

"For which of the Father's many gifts did you ask, Rachel?" She was like a piece of alabaster, precious and transparent.

"I asked for the gift of listening. I don't think we listen to each other enough."

It was a time of silent prayer and I was grateful. What could I say to so much beauty? Let the Lord say it in

75

His way. The silence was the pregnant kind when the Spirit is so present He is almost palpable.

As we continued to praise the Lord, we moved on into the part of the service where we took communion. Father Richard's words had centered on the Father's forgiveness of each of us. His great love for us sent His Son to redeem us, each of us. "Bart, are you listening?" I thought.

When we got to the Kiss of Peace, I was beside a black boy whom I had never seen at the prayer meetings before.

"I'm Sister Gus. What's your name?"

"Toby," he answered softly.

I gave Toby the same kind of rib-cracking hug we all exchanged at the prayer meeting liturgies and his body stiffened. I couldn't decide if it was because I was a nun, or white, or female, or all three. So I smiled and moved on to the next person who happened to be Sam.

"Do you know him?" I asked Sam, motioning toward Toby.

"Yeah. He goes to school across the way. I'm surprised to see him here because he isn't Catholic."

"Try to make him feel welcome, Sam. I didn't get any response. He might be shy."

"Will do," was Sam's concerned reply.

As the liturgy ended, young people piled out in a great rush. The eternal curfew against which we battled. Bart was somewhere in the crowd. The press of bodies had edged me over into a corner beside a form slumped over. I recognized the jacket. It was Arkie and his shoulders were heaving up and down. Father Richard got to him at the same time.

"Richard, do you think this is a troubled soul? Can we help?"

"No, Gus, I think he's just too overjoyed to be able to talk just yet."

76

Father Richard and I stood quietly by Arkie waiting for a period of calm.

Without lifting his head and between sobs, Arkie said, "Why me? How could He be so good to me? Why me?"

"We can all ask the same question, Arkie. None of us really deserves all the gifts the Father gives us every day," I offered.

"But it was awful, Sister. It was during the Mass. When Father Rick was talking about the Father's forgiveness. I was sitting with my eyes closed and I saw the most awful things. Like war everywhere and people killing each other and starving babies and blood and death. It was awful. And it seemed as though someone was saying to me, 'This is what hell is like. And you make it yourself.' It was awful, awful."

Arkie's shoulders were heaving again and he was sobbing uncontrollably. I was kneeling at Arkie's feet and Father Richard reached over and put his arm around Arkie's shoulders and encouraged, "That's what it's all about, Arkie. The Father gave us a free will. We only have to choose His way."

After a few moments, Arkie was quiet again and lifted his head. He was smiling. "That's the next part of the vision, Father. All that awful stuff was wiped out when you said, 'I proclaim to you the Good News that you are forgiven.' It was like putting a 1000-watt bulb in a socket. Light everywhere. I've been such a creep. I wonder how He can be so good to me." The tears were coming again but Arkie was smiling now. Several of us gathered round him and prayed for his uplifting.

"Say, Arkie," Sam piped in. "You've got to get you a Scripture teaching to launch you off on your way as a new man. Go ahead. Open up that New Testament you've got there."

Arkie's hands were trembling as he opened his New Testament and read from Ephesians 3:16-19.

Out of his infinite glory, may he give you the power through his Spirit for your hidden self to grow strong, so that Christ may live in your hearts through faith; and then, planted in love and built on love, you will with all the saints have strength to grasp the breadth and the length, the height and the depth, until, knowing the love of Christ, which is beyond all knowledge, you are filled with the utter fullness of God.

"Hey, buddy, your work is cut out for you," Sam commented.

"The Lord is already doing great things in your life, Arkie. And He will do more if you let Him," I added.

"Let's just praise the Lord once again for what He's already done for you, Arkie," Father Richard injected, and we all burst into a joyous rendition of "Praise Him."

It was then I noticed Bart standing apart from us. His face was ashen and he was perspiring profusely, which seemed unusual because several windows were open to air out the room.

"Don't you feel well, Bart?" the nurse in me asked.

"Some fresh air will help. Also a good stiff drink."

"The fresh air I can supply. Let's head for home. Sara Kate and Molly will already be in the car most likely."

We waved our goodbyes and headed for the parking lot. Coming from the bright lights of the school out into the night, my eyes weren't in focus when I first noticed the young woman standing near my car. But I recognized that silhouette. It was the young girl from the monastery parking lot, Mimi. "Parking lots must be her official territory," I thought.

"Hi, Mimi," I greeted her without much enthusiasm. No reply. She stared past me as though I weren't even present. But her eyes didn't miss Bart.

"What a place for a gal on the make to hang out!" Bart snapped through his teeth. "A prayer meeting yet. She must be hard up."

"Bart, how can you make that kind of judgment? She might be waiting for a friend."

"Don't give me any of that garbage, Gus. Anybody, you included, can look at that gal and know what she's up to. And it isn't passing out prayer leaflets, honey."

I don't know why I did it but I turned to Mimi and asked, "Do you need a ride, Mimi? We're going to North Bend and Colerain."

"You damn, stupid nun," she spit at me. It was the monastery parking lot scene all over again. She dashed away into the night. This time I knew for sure she was crying.

"That gal is right, Gus. Sometimes you are stupid," Bart offered. "Don't tell me you're going to try to convert her?"

"No, I'm not going to convert her. Jesus is."

"Now just a minute, Gus. I'll go along with your prayer meeting ritual since this seems to be what some kids need. But that babe that just ran off, she's made her road already. Nothing is going to change that. It's written all over her. The way she's dressed. The way she stands. The way she walks. She's selling her body. And she probably has already sold her soul to the devil. You're really off the track if you think you'll ever get through to her kind!"

"I repeat, Bart. I'm not going to get to her. Jesus is."

Bart muttered something unintelligible as he slammed the car door.

Sara Kate and Molly were singing softly in the back seat and Bart was silent all the way home. As I left him off at the apartment building, I cautioned, "Bart, have you had a physical exam lately?"

"So now I'll get the nurse routine?"

"Seriously, Bart, your color isn't good. Your breathing is shallow. And you were perspiring profusely back at the school with all the windows open. It's cold tonight."

"That was *my* response to your prayer meeting, Gus. Like you said, we all respond differently. That priest friend of yours, what's his name, really needled me with all that forgiveness line."

"Don't you think you need forgiveness, Bart?"

"Look, Gus, you live your life the way you want to, and I'll live mine the way I want to. We only get one chance at it and I don't want to miss anything. Got it?"

"I do, Bart."

Bart sauntered toward his apartment building still breathing fire, still erect and militant. I headed toward Molly's home as Sara Kate commented with wisdom, "He really doesn't know that his life is empty, does he?"

"Let's pray for Mr. Newcomb right now," Molly suggested.

And so we prayed in the midst of the sounds of night traffic and police sirens. We prayed for Mimi, too. I felt a great peace about them both even though they seemed eons away from ever knowing the Lord Who died for them.

"Molly, it's past eleven. Let me come in with you and explain to your mother why we're late," I offered.

"No, Sister," she replied so quickly. "Some way my mother has to learn to trust me. I shouldn't have to produce evidence to prove that my being late is legitimate. Thanks anyway."

As Sara Kate and I waited in the car until Molly got in her front door I said a quiet prayer that her mother would be understanding. It was a short distance to Sara Kate's home. Strange how they had lived two blocks apart for seventeen years and yet had never met until the prayer meetings.

Sara Kate asked hesitantly, "Who was that girl in the parking lot back at Our Lady of Angels, Sister Gus?"

"I don't know anything about her except that her name is Mimi. That might not even be her name but that is the name she gave me the first time I met her in the parking lot by the monastery."

"Is it true what Mr. Newcomb said, that she's a prostitute?"

"I don't know that either, Sara Kate. She's run off both times I've spoken to her. Say, why don't you and I make a covenant right now? Would you want to pray and fast for Mimi and Mr. Newcomb this week?"

"You've got a deal, Sister Gus. I've never tried to fast before but I want to do it."

As Sara Kate bounded up the sidewalk of her home, I praised the Lord again for the transformation He had brought about in this young woman.

"And someday, Lord, if You please, Mimi and Bart, too!"

7. Stay Loose

February 11, 1972 dawned bleak and gray, with a misty sleet falling to snarl the morning traffic. The big day of our appointment with the Archbishop had arrived after months of postponing the inevitable. We'd realized for a long time we had to find a bigger place to hold the prayer meetings. Inescapable, too, was the possibility of our being called before the Archbishop to be queried about the "happenings" at the TEC retreats and prayer meetings. The rumor factory had been working overtime.

Chugging along in a '65 Chevy with one door bashed in, Richard and I didn't seem a very impressive delegation to be presented to an Archbishop. But we did have an impressive backing. Promises of prayerful support had come from a variety of sources and denominations and this gave us the courage we needed to present our case. Some were fasting. Several had an all-night prayer vigil. So many believed in us. And many dubbed us kooks.

To the accompaniment of the blaring horns of impatient drivers, Richard and I started to pray together for a special outpouring of the Holy Spirit on our forthcoming meeting. As we neared the Seventh Street exit of Interstate 75, I asked for a Scripture teaching and opened my Bible to 1 Chronicles 28:20–21 and read:

"Be strong, stand firm; be fearless, be dauntless and set to work, because Yahweh God, my God, is with you. He will not fail you or forsake you before you have finished all the work to be done for the house of Yahweh. Here are the orders of priests and Levites for all the duties of the house of God; every willing man of any aptitude will help you in all this work; the officials and all the people are entirely at your command."

The Word left us breathless. I squealed in the sheer joy of feeling the Lord's comfort and encouragement so powerfully in His Word. We didn't dream how prophetic these words of Scripture were to be for us.

Still in high key as we cruised into a parking space right in front of the Chancery, I literally shouted, "Richard, do you realize this means *us—now—*the Archbishop and all the people will be with us. It says so right here in the Word!"

But Richard was intent in getting the '65 Chevy parked without another battle scar, and finally managed a "Yeah, that's great" half-whispered reply. How good the Lord was to have provided us with one single parking slot right in front of the Chancery office! Standing in the mist of that February morning my momentary exhilaration was overshadowed by the more mundane problem of producing the right coins for the parking meter.

This was my first visit to the Chancery office in Cincinnati. From a woman's point of view, I was acutely aware of the furnishings. I had expected it to be plush. In reality the furnishings were drab and worn. The only bit of color was provided by a large floral arrangement. Plastic. We announced ourselves to a prim secretary who informed us the Archbishop was busy with another appointment. "Please wait here," was her terse directive.

Waiting is never easy, particularly for two such naturally impatient characters as Richard and I. Though neither of us actually voiced our thoughts on waiting, we both felt disappointment, fearing that this would cut a chunk out of the time we would have with the Archbishop. Every minute was precious to convey our message and hopes. Yes, and our dreams, too.

In our prayer we had agreed that we wouldn't have any planned presentation. We claimed the scripture in Luke 12:11–12 which says: "Do not worry about how to defend yourselves or what to say, because when the time comes, the Holy Spirit will teach you what you must say." We would be supple in the hands of the Spirit.

Archbishop Paul Francis Leibold appeared in the doorway wearing a red-trimmed cassock opened at the neck sans Roman collar. I'd never seen him without all his ceremonial regalia. He looked tired and ashen but his smile of greeting was warm and his handshake firm. For the first time in my life I realized an Archbishop is truly a human being like the rest of us. Our meeting with him would cement that fact in my mind as he searched and suffered with us.

After the brief preliminary banter, Archbishop Leibold zeroed in on his primary concern as he directed his query to Father Richard. "Tell me about your retreats for the teen-agers."

Scooting forward on his chair to accent his sincerity, Father Richard launched off on one of his favorite topics. "We bring these kids together from schools in Ohio and Kentucky to search with them through darkness and shadows into the light. As a team we try to help them make that leap of faith when they can let Jesus take over their life. No gimmicks. No sophisticated audiovisuals.

I preach Jesus! The kids are desperately searching for a real Person to whom they can relate right here and now."

"We meet this situation all the time," I interrupted. "On the last retreat I asked a high school senior what she knew about Jesus. And her answer was, 'Nothing!' I prodded her on. 'After 12 years of Catholic school, how can you say you don't know anything about Jesus?'

"She looked at me hard with that familiar you-nuns-are-never-with-it expression. Do you know what we get in high school religion class? I'll tell you. We get the Pill, abortion, sex, war, racism, and that stuff. I haven't heard anything about Jesus since I was in grade school and then it was so icky sweet, I couldn't stand it. So I told you the truth when I said I didn't know anything about Jesus.' And she sashayed down the hall."

Father Richard picked the conversation up again. "In addition to this aspect of our Catholic kids' not knowing Jesus in a personal way, we have another factor with which we battle. Namely, the kids who are making the retreat because they *have* to make one. Their school makes this policy, otherwise, they don't receive a diploma. So they come with the attitude I'm-here-because-I-have-to-be. In most cases, it's a flop. They gain nothing from the three days and unfortunately pull others down with them."

My own enthusiasm for the whole concept of the TEC retreats and their potential couldn't be contained. "Even with the drawbacks," I bubbled, "when we put Jesus in the center, fantastic things begin to happen!"

The Archbishop looked at me placidly and commented, "Perhaps it would be well if we talked of some of those happenings."

"You've probably already heard of our famous November boys' TEC," Richard began, shifting his position in a creaky armchair. "Some of the boys making that

85

retreat were star jocks from a local high school, not the type given to emotionalism or piety or anything religious. During the retreat some of them came to a point of real powerful conversion. They wanted to know Jesus in a more personal way and they do!"

"Just what would you say that entails?" asked the Archbishop in an even tone.

"For these young men it meant a natural response of wanting to share their new-found Christian joy," explained Father Richard. "Yet at every turn they were met with criticism and outright hostility. This is in a *Catholic* high school! They were told they couldn't go around carrying a Bible or wearing a cross on the outside of their shirt. And above all, absolutely no prayer meetings!"

Directing his next question at me, the Archbishop asked, "Would you tell me about the prayer meetings, Sister?"

"I wish you would share one with us! We started just three months ago with twelve kids who were interested as a follow-up for the TEC retreats. Now we have wall-to-wall teen-agers and need a bigger place to meet. We come together to praise God and end the evening with a communion celebration. There are Scripture readings, much singing, silent prayer and spontaneous prayer. When you put Jesus in the center as Lord, He takes care of it all!" Now *I* was on the edge of my chair.

The Archbishop was silent for a time and seemed to be thinking aloud when he commented, "I wish more priests and religious in this Archdiocese would put Jesus in the center of their lives." After another quiet time, he asked Father Richard the question we had hoped to avoid.

"In what you have both been telling me, I'd say you

have a bit of the Cursillo plus a leaning toward pentecostalism. Would you say this is true, Father?"

My mouth felt suddenly like a desert but Father Richard fielded the question with confidence, a confidence that comes with claiming the scripture that the Holy Spirit will provide the words.

"Yes, it is true, Archbishop Leibold. But we didn't start out that way. We began the TEC retreats the same way they'd been done for years. When we moved into areas of shared prayer, the Spirit obviously wanted to lead us in a different way and He did. Now that the prayer meetings are tending to a more pentecostal..type prayer, there is no turning back. As Sister has said, Jesus is in the center and He calls the shots."

For some moments the Archbishop shared with us his great concern for the young, so many of whom are leaving the church. It was apparent that here was a man, designated by Rome to be shepherd of the flock of the Archdiocese of Cincinnati, deeply pained by the church's evident lack of success in keeping the young in the church. In a most serious mood he said, "I wonder if you two realize what a gift you have to be able to speak to young people. I can't."

I was dumbfounded. This was an Archbishop speaking, an Archbishop who had just grown ten feet tall in stature in my mind. His statement was a jolt to me. I had never thought of our ministry to youth as a special "gift." But at that moment I took time out to praise Jesus and thank Him for the gift. And most of all to thank Him for the gift of such a man as the Archbishop. It is a true measure of wisdom to recognize our limitations as well as our gifts.

Faintly I heard the bells of the Cathedral ringing the noon Angelus and realized we had been with the Archbishop for nearly two hours. That's phenomenal when

87

you think of his busy, tight schedule—an added indication of his great concern for youth. Before leaving, he promised he'd make available for our TEC retreats and prayer meetings some larger facility in the Archdiocese. The Archbishop said this with such certainty I knew he meant to do it and soon.

Buoyed up by the past hours, we zoomed homeward in silence too filled with prayerful gratitude to be able to speak. Father Richard returned to the monastery and shared his excitement with Brother Mark, an effervescent young man. As Richard rushed off to pick up Brother Dennis, Brother Mark went to the chapel to praise the Lord for His great kindness. When he opened his Scripture at random, his Bible fell open to 1 Chronicles 28:20–21! "Be strong, stand firm; be fearless, be dauntless and set to work, because Yahweh God, my God, is with you."

Later in the day when Father Richard returned to the monastery and was at prayer, he opened his Bible to read the Word and it fell open to 1 Chronicles 28:20–21! Such a powerful confirmation could only come from a loving Jesus Who so wants to give gifts to His people if we only ask! But this was only the beginning of an incredible day.

When I got back to my convent, I was limp from the events of the morning. I flopped on my bed and planned to reconstruct our conversation with the Archbishop. Instead I fell asleep and something that never happens to me at midday occurred. I had a dream, so vivid it is still etched in my memory.

I always dream in color. In my dream it was as though I were looking through a lens of a giant camera. The camera was recording a pan shot of countless numbers of young people. Some faces I recognized. Many were strangers. But they were all joyful, happy young faces—

black, white, yellow, tan. The camera zoomed to the center of this vast throng. And there in the center stood Father Richard wearing his brown Franciscan habit, standing peacefully with his head bowed in prayer. I wakened suddenly and my face was wet with tears. The first thought that popped in my head was, "Jesus, is this where You're leading us?"

When I was fully awake, I prayed, "Jesus, teach me what this means." I opened my Scriptures and my eyes fell on 1 Chronicles 29:1, "My son, whom alone Yahweh has chosen, is young, of tender years, and the work is great."

To me, there was no doubt concerning the direction the Lord was moving in Father Richard's youth ministry.

"Jesus, if only we had a bigger place for the kids," I pleaded. The Archbishop had said, "Soon." But the Lord had other plans. Suddenly on June 1, 1972 at 57, Paul Francis Leibold was dead.

8. The Desert Wasteland

When I was a young girl growing up in the Pennsylvania hills, I conceived the whole world to be much the same as my surroundings. Geography classes helped broaden my perspective. But the real cosmic enlightenment came when I traveled the globe as a U. S. Navy flight nurse. There are many scenic wonders in the world but the one I found most impressive was the Sahara, perhaps because it was the absolute antithesis of my Pennsylvania hills.

On the North Africa run, we landed at the U. S. Naval Air Station, Port Lyautey, Morocco. My first flight into Port Lyautey was an unforgettable initiation. The landing was rough and when the Officer of the Day came aboard he announced that we would be grounded indefinitely "until the sirocco had blown out its fury." As I left the aircraft, my flight cap was ripped off my head by the force of the wind, and I never did find it again. I clung to the railing making my way down the steps. The sand stung my face and I tried to cover my eyes. There was sand in my mouth, my nose, my ears. The wind seemed to pick up the jeep and carry us airborne to the nurses' quarters. No point in trying to question the Arab driver. You couldn't shout above the sound of the wind.

Sand, sand, sand everywhere. It seeped in through the

chinks in the window, under the door. Sand in the bed, sand in the food, sand in the coffee. Amazing that an entire U. S. Naval Air Station could be paralyzed by a storm. Yet the sirocco had been around a long, long time before the U. S. Navy came into existence. Yearly the placid, still sands of the desert are transformed into a cataclysmic nightmare by the sirocco.

And when the storm is over, the beauty and mystery of the desert are even more breathtaking. The utter still-ness and aloneness of the desert impel you to whisper even in ordinary conversation. I was adventuresome, and hired an Arab guide plus camel. The most difficult part of the journey into the desert was trying to prevent the nausea that overpowered me caused by the smell of the moth-eaten camel on which I was riding.

As I think back on that safari into the Sahara, it re-minds me of prayer. Like prayer, it was a movement constantly toward surprise. The surprise of encounter around every dune. Would there be someone else out there on the desert? Perhaps one of the desert brigands about whom I had read so many tales? Or a member of the French Foreign Legion? I had met several of them at the Officers Club . . . astringent, bristling men. Perhaps I might even meet Antoine de Saint Exupéry's "Little Prince" or some of his friends.

But there was no one else. Only sand and sun and my smelly camel. I had no sense of direction. To the east, north, south, west, the desert looked the same—the un-ending undulations of the dunes. I had full trust in my Arab guide. He had agreed we would turn around in time to get back to the base before sundown. We made it at dusk.

Now some years later in Cincinnati, Ohio as a Glen-mary Sister, I was experiencing "desert" in quite another manner—the spiritual wasteland of the desert. Like the

Sahara, this desert, too, is mysterious, lonely, unpredictable, uncharted.

It was February 16, 1972—Ash Wednesday. Father Richard had finished a Scripture class for the kids and some of them asked if we could have a prayer meeting following the class. We stayed on at the TEC Lodge, gathered a few candles, and sat on the floor. From the beginning of the prayer meeting, there seemed to be some sort of oppression. When we sang, the usual scintillation was missing. The spontaneous prayers were draggy and morose. The gospel for the coming Sunday came to mind —Jesus' temptation in the desert, important enough for three evangelists to include it in their Gospels. Like being back in the Sahara: groping, trusting in a guide. *The* Guide, Jesus, to bring us out of the desert.

From the TEC office came sounds of violent sobbing. I was tempted to run toward the sobs and embrace whoever it might be but an invisible something seemed to indicate I shouldn't move. A quick visual check around the room registered the fact that Ziggy and Father Richard were missing. Nothing could be that sad to cause such sobbing. Why Ziggy? He'd been walking the deeper life of the Spirit for several months. Then it clicked. What better target for the Devil than someone who is hungry for the Word of God and for a deeper walk?

My awareness was shattered again by the sound of weeping much closer to me. It was vibrant, bouncy Phyllis. She was drooped over like a daisy with a shattered stem. I put my arms around her to ease some of the desperation. I could hear in her cry and feel in her body the desolation of a crushed spirit.

"What's the matter with me, Sister Gus?" Phyllis muttered between sobs. "It's such a piercing, awful sensation inside. Weird. I've never had anything like this happen to me before—not since my mother told me I'd been an accident. I feel so all alone. Nothing to grab on to—"

Several of us drew close around Phyllis to support her in prayer. I couldn't believe my eyes and ears. The same thing was happening to others in the prayer group, too. The desert on a sweeping scale. How like the Old Fox to throw us into a panic!

Over the top of Phyllis's head, Sam was in my line of vision. He seemed so fidgety, quite unlike his usual manner. On his face emblazoned for all to view was an expression of let's-get-this-over-with. Sam was ordinarily the last one wanting to terminate a prayer meeting.

Jazz, with his artist's temperament, was vacillating but I never had seen him like this. He was picking aimlessly at his guitar strings. Void of harmony or rhythm, the music was a total distraction.

Brother Dennis's voice boomed out, "Let's stand and praise the Lord. We can't let the devil take over like this. Let's praise the Lord."

Our praise started out falteringly but gradually grew in volume. Phyllis smiled a little. Ziggy and Father Richard were back and they joined in the singing. Jazz was accompanying the singing now. Sam's face was transformed by the words of praise.

When there was a time of silent prayer, Ziggy leaned over and whispered, "You ever been in the desert, Sister Gus? I'm a pro at it now."

I nodded that I understood, recalling spiritual deserts in my own life. None of us is ever a pro in the spiritual desert no matter how many times we endure such an experience. Each occurrence is unique. Each brings its own rock bottom and its own healing and grace and growth and lesson—if we permit it. The desert if never the same and never easy.

Phyllis had quietly moved up behind me and crushed

my ribs in a bear hug. Such a lovable young lady. How could anyone, much less her own mother, tell her she was an accident? Her parents claimed the same mailing address but that's the only thing they seemed to share these days.

"I'm so glad I've got you to love, Sister Gus," Phyllis whispered in my ear.

"You've got the whole wide world to love, Phyllis."

"Not me. You get hurt too bad that way. I take people just one at a time. That's all I can handle."

"That's true. Sometimes we do get hurt," I answered. "But the risk is worth it all when love is returned—without measure, running over."

"This is still new to me. You have to give me time to get used to being able to love. The only thing I really knew how to do when I came to that first prayer meeting was how to hate!"

"Phyllis, did you ever think that maybe the reason Jesus came into your life was to reach your parents?"

"I don't get you."

"With Jesus' love, you can learn to love your parents."

"They don't care about my love. They just don't care about anything I do."

"Have you told them about the Scripture class and prayer meetings, Phyllis? Don't they want to know where you are on Wednesday and Friday nights?"

"No," she answered firmly. "So long as I stay out of their way, everything is fine. As soon as I start asking questions or trying to talk to Mom or Dad, they have something else to do right then."

"Phyllis, why don't we ask the community here to pray with us for your folks?"

"Sister Gus, I know you mean well but it would be a drag. My folks don't care. I really am an accident to them, always have been."

"You are not an accident, Phyllis. With God our Father, there are no accidents. Repeat: *there are no accidents*. You are *His* child."

"I guess I don't have that kind of faith yet to believe God could change my parents."

"He changed you, didn't He?"

"Wow! Did He? Yeah, He took over."

"So let's step out in faith and ask Him to do the same for your parents."

"Could just you and I do it, Sister Gus? I don't want to bring all this stuff up in front of everybody here."

"We're all in this together. That's the whole point of a praying community. We sustain each other. No one here is going to judge you or your parents. We're going to lift them up to the Lord and ask Him to move in."

"But I don't know what to say."

"The Spirit will give you the words to say. Just open your mouth and let them come out. Keep your eyes on Jesus. He's the center. Nobody else here can claim that spot. Hang loose and let it come."

We were all standing now, holding hands in a giant circle, as we sang the "Our Father." Phyllis was on one side of me and Ziggy on the other. As we finished the "Amen," Phyllis gripped my hand so hard my fingers hurt. And then she began to sing in the Spirit in a lovely tone, the kind that should have a dulcimer accompanying it. Her face was uplifted and shining. Other voices joined hers, a polyphony of sound in perfect harmony rising to a great crescendo and then subsiding gently.

This was the kind of magic moment you want prolonged forever. But such was not meant to be. The door of the TEC Lodge was opposite from where I was standing and leaning against it was the bulk of Chesty. His name was so appropriate in describing his anatomy. Star highschool jock, Chesty had the swagger of one who is

95

accustomed to female adulation and male envy. When he made a boys' TEC, he resisted so strongly that he became physically ill. Some weeks after that, he came to a prayer meeting for kicks. With some other jocks, he had planned to create an uproar at the prayer meeting and "show it up for the phony it was" in his words. That particular night, Jesus had other plans. He planted Toby right beside Chesty.

Gradually Toby had overcome his reticence to be himself at the prayer meetings. He was blossoming slowly and genuinely. Now he returned the Kiss of Peace and mingled with the crowd rather than standing off in a corner. Toby was a star jock in his own right, but Chesty was the captain of the football team and there was an evident mutual admiration between them.

Chesty clapped Toby on the back in greeting and said, "Say, Toby, I never expected to see you at one of these meetings."

"Likewise, man," Toby replied with equanimity. "First time you're here?"

"Yeah. We came to stir up a little action."

"Then you've come to the wrong place, man, unless you mean the action is prayer," asserted Toby.

"Hey, I don't believe what I'm hearing. You mean you dig this prayer stuff, Toby? Like it's for real?"

"It's for real, man."

"You gotta be out in orbit to be talking like this, Toby."

"That's the straight scoop, man. And if that's why you came, great. If it's not, man, you'd better split. You can get your action some place else where the booze is flowing free and the pot comes easy."

"I thought you was my soul brother, Toby."

"I am your soul brother, man. That's why I'm telling you like it is, see?"

"Who's to stop us from rearranging the place?"

"Nobody will stop you, Chesty. They'll just start praying over you. They'll get you like they got me. And since I'm standing right here beside you, I'd probably be the first one to pray over you. Are you ready for that?"

"Holy cow, I'm getting out of this joint. You're a bunch of creeps!"

Chesty did depart hurriedly that night. But a week later he was back. He found a spot on the opposite side of the room from Toby. During the prayer meeting he stood, leaning against the wall, seemingly impassive. But when we came to the penitential rite of the Mass, he was kneeling, doubled over with his head on the floor. It was the position of a man in agony, wanting so much to be forgiven and yet doubting that the Lord really would forgive him. But the power of the Lord is mighty and is meant for all men. As the Mass progressed, Chesty straightened to an upright kneeling position. His face was peaceful now.

At the kids' prayer meetings, the Kiss of Peace is always an adventure. This night was no exception. As I neared Chesty, I noticed that Toby had reached him first. It is heartening to me to see brother embrace brother in the sign of fraternal friendship and concern. Chesty literally caved in when Toby gave him a bear hug. I don't know what Toby said at that moment, but tears were rolling down Chesty's face. Externally, he didn't look much like a star jock just then. But he was a star—a radiant star in Jesus' crown.

Because of the transformation in his life style, Chesty had to cope with a lot more static than most. As an all-round star in the sports arena, he was in the public eye. His team mates couldn't assimilate the change. When Chesty removed his sweat jersey and some sharp-eye noticed he was wearing a cross, the locker room was in an uproar. Another day when Chesty opened his locker, a stack of books fell out with a New Testament among them, and some of his team mates dubbed him "preacher." But Chesty stayed with it, sustained by the fellowship of the prayer meetings.

Now, several months later on this Ash Wednesday night, he was leaning against the wall in the same stance as he had when he first began his walk in the Spirit. I started to move toward him to welcome him and I didn't want to believe what my eyes were seeing. Perhaps the candlelight was deceptive. But there was no mistake. A girl had entered TEC lodge and gently placed her hand on Chesty's arm. Before I reached him, the two had walked out. The girl was *Mimi!*

Mysterious Mimi. Hungry for love wherever she could find it, no matter how fleeting. So many questions were beating into my brain. How had they met? Was it friendship or client-customer relationship? Was Chesty being whisked away from the prayer community by the feminine wiles of Mimi? Or had Chesty seen beyond the facade of ultra-sophistication to the real Mimi?

The prayer meeting was breaking up. Sam called to me as he scooted past, "Hey, Sister Gus, come join us at the pizza parlor. A lot of the kids are going there."

"Sam, my gall bladder does flips when anyone even mentions pizza."

"They serve other stuff, too. See you there. OK?"

"OK, Sam. I'll come for a little while."

"Now you've done it," I thought. "Why did you promise to go to the pizza parlor?"

So true. A pizza parlor is the last place in the world I wanted to be right then. But something was urging me on to go there, so I entered the mainstream of traffic going up Colerain Avenue. I wondered where Chesty and Mimi were at that moment.

I didn't have to wonder long. Several of us arrived at the same time at the pizza parlor and as we entered, I noticed a group of our kids had already cordoned off a group of tables. Sitting at one of the tables were Chesty and Mimi. Chesty waved for me to join them. I was in a fog as I walked toward their table.

Mimi's appearance startled me. With her blond hair pulled back in a pony tail, wearing flares and a smock top, she looked fresh and sparkling. And miracle or miracles, she smiled.

"Sister Gus, you're going to have to help us eat a king-size pizza," Chesty invited.

"He insisted on ordering the biggest one in the place," Mimi commented.

Though pizza and my digestive system don't get along very well, I knew this was one night my gastric function would be sacrificed. This was a precious fellowship opportunity I didn't intend to miss.

I felt the presence of Jesus so strongly here in the pizza parlor. How incongruous! Yet, why should I be surprised? All my life, in unmistakable, definite, special ways, Jesus has touched me. He comes and goes whenever He chooses, usually it seems, just to let me know He cares—He is with me. He loves me and loves other persons who are close to Him like Chesty and maybe Mimi, too.

The smell of cheese and garlic from the pizza, the largest I had ever seen, was pungent. That plus the background noises of any such eating place, seemed an unusual atmosphere for prayer but I found myself praying.

"Jesus, let Your love and power touch the hearts and minds of these young people I talk with tonight or those who simply see me. You have power over them, Lord, not I. Open their hearts to receive Your love and peace. Especially Mimi."

Between bites from the pizza, Chesty remarked, "Golly, I'm sorry I had to miss the Scripture class of Father Rick's and the prayer meeting tonight. Basketball practice."

"How about Friday night?" I asked.

"That's a big game. We play Elder High. And we've got to beat them this year."

"Come over after the game. You'll get there for part of the liturgy anyway. Bring Mimi."

"Maybe some other time," Mimi remarked.

"Yeah, basketball season will be over soon and then we can come," Chesty agreed.

Bluntly I decided to put my cards on the table and launched out with the comment, "I was surprised to see you two together tonight."

"Why should that surprise you, Sister Gus?"

"I didn't think you did any heavy dating during basketball season."

"Jeez, Sister Gus. I like dames. I don't think a guy has to swear off altogether. I follow all the rules. The coach is happy. I'm happy."

With deliberateness, Mimi looked square at me and asked, "What you really mean is that you didn't expect to see Chesty with *me*. Isn't that right?"

I could feel the blood rising to my face and I was sure I must be crimson. The steel was back in Mimi's eyes.

Truth is always the best answer and in truth, I answered, "Yes, Mimi, that is what I meant."

"Don't you think I'm good enough for Chesty?" she snapped.

"Hey, doll, cool it! What are you getting so huffy about?" Chesty asked.

Mimi was an attractive young woman; no doubt about

it. And in her anger she seemed even lovelier when the anger smoldered in her eyes. Looking at her, I could imagine an even more beautiful Mimi—one on fire with the love of Christ. Something deep within me was urging me to stick to the task of following through with the truth, even if Mimi spit in my eye and Chesty exploded.

Looking into Mimi's face, hardened into a mask of self-defence, I said, "I'll tell you both precisely what I'm thinking. I've seen you twice before tonight, Mimi. In both instances, it has been in a parking lot and you've called me a damn, stupid nun. From the way you were dressed, the way you stood, the way you walked, your response to my greeting, I pegged you as a gal on the make—maybe even a professional prostitute. From way back in my student nurse days working in the V. D. Clinic, I learned one fact about prostitutes: they are desperately hungry for love, even if they have to sell their bodies to try to get it. But you don't have to sell your body, Mimi. Chesty isn't that kind of guy."

Chesty was staring at me with his mouth open as though about to speak but the words wouldn't come. Mimi's face had crumpled and tears were rolling down her pale cheeks. Silently I was praying for the right words to continue when Toby sat down at our table.

"Hey, man," Toby began in his usual effervescent way, "How come everybody at this table looks so serious?"

"We were having a rather serious discussion," I remarked.

"Well, I don't mean to interrupt but I wanted to meet Chesty's date. So I barged in. OK?"

"Yeah, man," Chesty replied in a half whisper. "Toby, this is my friend, Mimi. Mimi, I want you to meet a great guy, Toby."

"Hi," was all Mimi could get out as she reached for a Kleenex.

"Sure nice to meet you, Mimi. Don't fall for the snow job this guy will give you. Be seeing you all." And Toby was gone, off to another table, bubbly and so enthusiastic about his new-found relationship with Jesus.

"Toby is right, Mimi. We *are* glad to meet you," I continued. "We're glad to meet you as the Mimi you really are, not as the Mimi you might appear to be because of exterior circumstances. I don't know anything about you, Mimi. And I don't have to know anything about you to love you. What I said to you in the parking lot up by the monastery the first time I saw you still goes: what you need, Mimi, is Jesus. His love for you is greater than any man's can ever be. Chesty has already begun a deeper walk in the Spirit and he can help you follow that way, too. We do love you, Mimi, if you'll let us. And even if you won't let us. Sometimes that happens when a gal has been hurt and doesn't feel she can ever trust anyone again."

"I'm not too sure I know exactly what all this is about, Sister Gus," Chesty interrupted. "I met Mimi in the parking lot, too, and asked her to come join us. Something just told me to do that and I did. I'm glad I did. There's something about her that makes a guy glad to be a guy. You know what I mean?"

"Yes, I know what you mean, Chesty. And I praise the Lord that He used you to bring Mimi closer to Him."

Mimi's eyes were red and she was on her third Kleenex when she spoke, "I'd like to tell you both to go to hell but somehow I can't do it. It was so easy to tell people to go hell before I met Chesty. I look at you, Sister Gus, and I know you mean what you say. But I hate nuns, do you understand? I hate nuns and everything you say, I want to tell you to stick it up your—. Sorry, even though I hate nuns, all of a sudden, I can't say it—"

"Mimi," I said meaning all the tenderness my voice was

102

expressing, "Believe me when I say I understand. I received my nurses' training under nuns who never spoke and never smiled and never gave student nurses any credit for having even a few brain cells functioning. I wanted to put every nun in that category. And I did for years until I was a Navy flight nurse during the Korean War and I met a nun in a bombed-out orphanage in Seoul, Korea. She was a Daughter of Charity. 'God's geese' the world used to call them, because of their headgear. All the rest of her community had left when the North Koreans started to move south. But this Sister stayed on. She was American-born and had that streak of stick-to-it-ive-ness that has made America a nation of pioneers. She didn't even have shoes the day I met her; she'd given them to one of the orphans. I came to the orphanage with a group of Marines—rough, tough, battle-seasoned Marines. But even the toughest of them couldn't resist the charm of those Oriental children or the woman who loved them so much she had elected to stay, knowing very well that she could be captured by the enemy and executed. And would you believe that it was on that day, amid all the hell of war in Korea, that I decided I wanted to be just like that woman—a woman given completely to the Lord and His work. Wherever it would be. Someday you're going to meet such a person, too, Mimi, who mirrors the love of Jesus so much that you know it's the only way to go."

The pizza parlor seemed uncommonly quiet. Most of the kids had gone and the proprietor was standing near the cash register as though hinting that we should be gone, too. Chesty caught my eye just about then and started to help Mimi on with her coat.

"Sister Gus," Chesty began, "I'm sure glad you came to join us."

"Chesty, the Lord has put it on my heart to say just

103

one more thing. But let's do that out by the car because I think this good man wants to close for the night."

"Right on," was Chesty's comment as he paid the check and we started for our cars, the last in the parking lot.

Mimi seemed more diminutive than ever in her fur-lined parka. She was very quiet but her body seemed relaxed as she leaned against Chesty's car. I looked at both these young people with a love so deep that I felt I would burst as I spoke.

"Mimi—Chesty" I began, shivering although the night wasn't that cold. "I get the feeling we've covered a lot of territory tonight. And I know, deep down in my bones, that Jesus is very much with us at this moment. We can only give what we've got. I can only tell you what I myself have experienced. And I know Jesus loves you. Just as you are. Not as somebody else in some other place—but as Mimi and Chesty right here in Cincinnati, Ohio. I lift you up to Jesus. He will work wonders in your life. If you let Him."

I embraced Mimi. Chesty almost cracked my ribs in returning my hug. They sped off into the night as I waited for my car to warm up a bit. I looked up toward the night sky studded with stars and I was overwhelmed with the realization of the power of God, creator of the universe—creator of the solar system and beyond the solar system. Universe—the term blows my mind. How great a God to have power over all these things that our minds in their finiteness can't even comprehend—and yet He has care for me. And Mimi. And Chesty. And everybody.

"Jesus," I prayed as I pulled out of the parking lot, "I lift them up to You. Take care of Mimi and Chesty. Help them lead each other to a deeper love of You in each other. Thaw them out!"

The night sky of Cincinnati was never more splendidly star-studded. So like nights in the Sahara.

9. Now Power

"They're going to let us do it, Sister Gus. Can you believe it? They're really going to let us do *Damn Yankees* with the guys from Roger Bacon. Whew!" Rachel's squeal of delight trailed off as she ran on ahead to share the news with others coming for the Wednesday night Scripture class.

That particular bit of news surprised me. My recollection of the Broadway version of *Damn Yankees* didn't seem to coincide with the qualities you would expect in a high school musical. I could still remember quite plainly Lola's sensuous solo, "Whatever Lola Wants, Lola Gets." Since that had been my own motto for a number of years as a Navy flight nurse, it wasn't unusual that I still recalled it. In these days of satanic cults and worship, *Damn Yankees* would be very contemporary with Mr. Appleby exhibiting his prowess in the misty realms of Satan's domain.

After the Scripture class, Brother Dennis filled me in on his upcoming adventure of helping to direct the musical. For some time he had wanted to do a musical with the high school kids rather than the usual concert. He felt the choice of *Damn Yankees* was a good one, since it was contemporary and diversified enough to provide a challenge for those who would be trying out for the parts.

"I have a feeling this is going to be something special,"

Brother Dennis confided. "We start tryouts Friday and I'm really excited about it."

"Too bad I'm not in high school," I mused. "I'd like to try out for Lola's part."

"Say, wouldn't that be a sensation? I can see the headlines," Brother Dennis teased. " 'Local Nun Stars in Musical Production.' That would be great."

"You dreamer. I'll be lucky if I can even attend as a member of the audience. Seriously, though, if you need any help, let me know."

"I'll tell you where you can help starting right now. Let's lift the whole thing up to the Lord in prayer. There's such a great potential in anything like this for the guys and gals to work together. They need leaders. And some of their natural enthusiasm just might rub off on some others who are asleep at the switch. So pray with me that this endeavor might work toward the glory of the Lord."

"Count on it, Brother Dennis. I'll recruit others from the prayer circle, too. This is part of the Body ministry, too."

"Thanks, Gussie. We'll see you get a front row seat!"

Our discussion was interrupted by Rachel with a new girl in tow. Alabaster Rachel is how I thought of this lovely young woman. She was translucent. Her movements were so delicate.

"I want you to meet my friend, Sylvia," Rachel began. "She's a senior at Colerain High and this is the first time she's come to the Scripture class. Help me talk her into coming to the prayer meeting on Friday."

Brother Dennis and I acknowledged the introduction. Sylvia seemed uneasy but not shy. Her black eyes and hair fit with her name. As in the song, "Sylvia's hair is like the night."

"How did you find out about the Scripture class, Sylvia?" I asked.

"All the kids at Colerain are talking about it. They were telling me about this groovy priest who tells it like it is and makes the Bible come alive. This I had to see and hear. I never have been able to get very interested in the Bible. So I came tonight to see for myself."

"Do you think your friends were right about the Scripture class?" Brother Dennis asked.

"Yeah. I know what they mean now. I just never heard anybody talk like this about Jesus before. Father Rick sounds like he really knows Jesus. You know, not an out-of-a-textbook kind of thing, but for real. And the way he talks about St. Paul, I think I would have liked knowing St. Paul. Father Rick makes him seem like somebody I could look up to as a hero. We don't have any heroes these days it seems," Sylvia ended on a thoughtful note.

How right she was! Where were the heroes? To whom could the young people look for inspiration and dedication? Somehow our generation was letting them down. Yet to me it seemed so clear: the only hero for young or old who had endured through the centuries was Jesus.

"Sylvia, in your opinion, what makes a hero?" I asked.

"Gee, Sister Gus, I don't know if I can put it into words how I feel about a hero. He's somebody who believes very strongly in what is right and lives his life that way. He's not afraid to stick his neck out for what he believes even if he gets clobbered. He's at home with the little man as well as with the great. And he listens. Not just to the words people say but even more to what they're not saying out loud. Does that sound like an impossible dream to think there is such a person?"

"There is such a person, Sylvia, and He is as close as your next word," I assured her.

"Come with me Friday, Syl, and learn more about what Sister Gus is saying," Rachel offered. Her eyes were sparkling.

"That's when they have the tryouts for *Damn Yankees* and I don't want to miss them."

"The prayer meeting doesn't start until 9 P.M. You'll be finished by then. Besides, I'm going to the tryouts, too. So is Brother Dennis. We can all go to the prayer meeting together afterwards. What do you say, Syl?"

"Let me think about it. I'll let you know tomorrow. I've got to get home now or my Mom will never let me out another night this week if I'm too late. See you." Sylvia and Rachel ran off to the parking lot as Brother Dennis and I exchanged "goodnights" and went our separate ways.

Sylvia's remarks about the Scripture class and heroes were churning in my mind during the drive home. The kids really were hungry for the Word of God, yet they weren't receiving the kind of nourishment they needed in their churches or homes. There were a few exceptions, pitifully few. Scripture truly is exciting, as the kids find out once they seek the Lord's teaching in His Word.

I could gather from the rumblings among the kids that the tryouts for *Damn Yankees* were very important to them. The lead parts were challenging and the chorus parts could be fun even if a lot of practice was needed. Plus all the background jobs that had to be done to bring a production off. Team work can accomplish miracles. I experienced an undercurrent of excitement every time I thought about the production. Perhaps the miracles wouldn't all be concerned with stage production! And there would be miracles!

When the kids arrived for the prayer meeting on Friday night, they were exploding. I caught bits and snatches of animated conversation until I could pin one down long enough to get a play-back of the tryouts.

"How did the tryouts go, Mitch?" I asked above the general din.

"Out of sight, man! You wouldn't believe all the guys and gals that showed up. It was great. We applauded like crazy for every one of them. I don't know how Brother Dennis ever made a decision for those parts."

"Will any of the kids from our prayer meeting be in the cast? I know some of them planned to go for the tryouts."

"Some of them? I think the whole bunch was there. None of them got a lead part but most of the chorus are kids from the prayer meeting. If they sing out in *Damn Yankees* like they do here at the prayer meeting, they'll blow the audience out of the place! Hey, won't that be far out?"

Brother Dennis had just arrived and he was beaming. The tryouts must have been fruitful. So many of the kids were mobbing him trying to learn who would get the lead parts. In his masterful way, he quieted them all by beginning the opening hymn and another prayer meeting was underway.

I noticed Rachel coming in and Sylvia was with her. The kids describe the sensation as "vibes" and the vibes were certainly right when Sylvia walked by. I couldn't explain it in any other way except to say that I knew the Lord was going to do something tremendous in this young woman's life. In our brief meeting after Scripture class she hadn't mentioned whether or not she was Catholic. And it didn't matter. Some who came to these prayer meetings regularly were not Catholic. Some didn't belong to any established church.

At announcement time during the prayer meeting, Father Richard reminded the kids that a group would be going to St. Michael's church in Sharonville the following Sunday to witness to a group of CCD students and teachers. The witnessing activity of the young folks was increasing. They were so eager.

109

Brother Dennis nudged me and said, "Come with us Sunday?"

"Sounds inviting. I'll be there," I promised. "How much preparation do you think these CCD classes have had for our kind of witnessing?"

"If this CCD group is like most of them, they've had no preparation. That's why I get so charged up about introducing them to the charismatic movement. They haven't had a chance to pre-judge us or brand us as kooks before we ever get there," Brother Dennis observed.

It was time to take communion as I made a mental note to set Sunday morning aside for our witnessing date. And at that moment I began to lift up the CCD students and teachers of Sharonville to the Lord in prayer so that He would prepare their hearts for our meeting with them on Sunday. Saturday would be a fasting day offered for them. I prayed, too, that the Lord would give me the words to say. Coming in cold to a group can be a frightening proposition until you come to the time in your Christian life when you realize that it is the Lord's work and not yours; and just as He promised, He will supply the words. The very words that each person needs to hear.

On Sunday morning we met in the rain in front of the Monastery: five guys, five gals, Brother Dennis and I—twelve apostles! We hadn't planned that significant number since it was an open-ended invitation. The Lord had planned it. In two cars we made our way to Sharonville, got lost trying to find the church, and arrived just as CCD classes were to begin. We were to speak to the high school students and their teachers.

The atmosphere wasn't a very receptive one. I could feel the resentment of the students. No doubt most of them were there because their parents had badgered them into coming to CCD classes. The session was to be an hour long, Ralph had told us. We were free to use whatever format and material we wished.

Ralph was the lay director of the parish CCD program. I don't know that he had such an official title but that was his position. He was in his mid-forties, himself the father of several teen-agers. His concern for the young people was genuine. But I knew from his edginess that Ralph had a long way himself to go before he could give his life over to Jesus. Only then would his CCD program have any real power and fire.

One by one our guys and gals alternated, giving their testimonies of how they had come to know the Lord. Ziggy started off the group after a brief introduction by Brother Dennis. Molly and Phyllis were especially effective because they sparkled so. I looked from them to the girls in our CCD audience who were the same age, same middle-class background. Such a visible difference! Brother Dennis spoke of the charismatic movement, its history in America, and its history in Cincinnati. The teachers seemed particularly intent while Dennis was speaking. The students' faces were impassive and they were restless.

Jazz was with us and had planned to accompany us as we sang "Tough Love," for which he had written the music. He had only played two chords and a string broke on his guitar. Then like a bolt from the blue, Brother Dennis said, "Let's have a mini-prayer meeting. We know the songs well enough to do it without the guitar."

As soon as we began praising the Lord, that room was transformed. The prayer meeting was low-key. We twelve were oblivious to the students' and teachers' presence. We were deep in the Lord and what He wanted to teach us. The prayers were spontaneous and real. Jazz praised the Lord for breaking his guitar string so that he could praise Him in word instead of in song. Ziggy had a Scripture teaching from 3 John 1:3–6.

111

It was a great joy to me when some brothers came and told of your faithfulness to the truth, and of your life in the truth. It is always my greatest joy to hear that my children are living according to the truth. My friend, you have done faithful work in looking after these brothers, even though they were complete strangers to you. They are a proof to the whole church of your charity and it would be a very good thing if you could help them on their journey in a way that God would approve.

The hour hand was nearing eleven as we stood to sing "Rejoice in the Lord Always." It was only then that I realized we were in front of the CCD students. Ralph announced to the class, "I know some of you have rides home at this time. Others may want to stay to ask questions. Anyone is free to leave who wishes."

But no one left.

The kids were sitting immobile. One girl was obviously crying as she bounded forward, hugged Ziggy, and shouted, "You kids are so real. How can I be that way?"

Another lad muttered under his breath but loud enough for me to hear, "What a bunch of damn, dumb kooks!" But he didn't move to leave. He kept watching us exchange the Kiss of Peace. I walked over to him and asked his name.

"Max."

"I'm Sister Gus."

"Hi." Max continued to look at the floor.

"The Lord keep you a man of peace," I said to Max as I hugged him. He was astounded.

"What's all this hugging bit?" Max asked as he looked up at me for the first time.

"It's our way of showing that we're glad to see each other and we're glad to be brothers and sisters in the

Lord. Don't you hug your folks and your brothers and sisters at home?"

"Hell, no. They'd think I'd lost my marbles if I went around hugging anyone at home."

"Maybe you should surprise them and try it some day, Max. Like when you go home from church this morning. Sunday is a great day to rejoice in the Lord."

"Hey, are you a Catholic nun?" Max queried.

"Yes, indeed. I'm a Glenmary Sister. Our Motherhouse is on Colerain Avenue. Do you know where that is?"

"Yeah, I've been to Mount Airy Forest a lot bike riding. You don't sound like a Catholic nun, though."

"There really isn't any special way a Catholic nun sounds, Max. We're individuals. Not carbon copies."

At this time, Ralph joined us. "Could I speak with you a moment, Sister Gus?" Then to Max he said, "Glad you stayed, Max." It was then I realized Max was Ralph's son. The resemblance was obvious.

"Sister, you and Brother Dennis and these kids really are turned on. Are you always this way?"

"Ever since we let the Lord take over our lives, yes. It is the most natural thing in the world now to go from place to place and speak of the wonders the Lord is doing in our lives every day. And the more you speak of it or think of it, the more excited you become. It's a glorious adventure, this Christian life, if we only let it be so."

"It all sounds very Protestant to me—your vocabulary, your songs, the way you pray. Are you planning to leave the convent and the church?" Ralph was quite serious in his questioning. His dark eyes were intense and not peaceful.

"I hope you will someday come to understand the way we speak and sing and pray as Christian—not Protestant or Catholic. We address the Lord Jesus as Christians,

113

children of His Father, baptized with the fire and power of the Spirit."

"I have to admit to you, Sister Gus, that I didn't think the kids would pay much attention to what all of you had to say. What seems to have captured them was the mini-prayer meeting, as Brother Dennis calls it. Then they knew you were for real. You couldn't have faked your your way through that."

"The Lord knew precisely what they needed and what would reach them. Young people put great stress on sincerity. When they know Jesus is Lord of your life and not a facade or a special condition you put on for Sundays only, they listen. And if you came to our Friday night prayer meetings, you would see how many not only come to listen but come to stay and pray because they want to do it. They are hungry for the truth."

"You mean we've got Jesus freaks in the Catholic Church?" Ralph asked incredulously.

"Ralph, you may call them Jesus freaks if you like. Personally, I call them Jesus *people*. Thank God they're in the Catholic Church, too."

A look almost of pain clouded Ralph's face. His brow was creased and he kept fiddling with his Xavier University class ring on his left hand. I sensed that he wanted to say more, so I stood still.

Shaking his head, Ralph commented, "Where have I been? I can't believe what I'm hearing and seeing here this morning. And now you're telling me we have Jesus freaks in the Catholic church, too. I thought they were only down on Fountain Square or Vine Street. What's the church coming to?"

"It's coming to Jesus—Jesus as Lord. Which is where it always should have been. Pope John asked for a new Pentecost and we're getting it! The young people have

114

picked up the ball and are running with it. In many cases, they're leaving the rest of us behind in the dust."

"Are there many of these—what did you call them—Jesus folk?"

"Jesus people. They're wall-to-wall at our Friday night prayer meetings. Why don't you come and bring your class with you? We'd be glad to have you with us."

"I'll have to think about that," Ralph replied as Brother Dennis gave me the high sign that it was time to leave. We wanted to make it back to the monastery to catch the Community of Hope Mass.

"I didn't want to rush you off, Gussie," Dennis apologized, "but I wanted to get to this Mass. We have practice for our musical starting at one this afternoon."

"How's the musical coming? I've been wanting to get to a practice."

"Why don't you come today? Since it's Sunday none of the other kids or the top brass will be around. Just the cast and the stage hands."

"Thanks for the invite. I think I will."

We got back for the Community of Hope Mass at the monastery. My thoughts were still back at St. Michael's. I kept seeing Ralph's troubled expression and aching for him. Like so many other Catholics, he felt the church was falling apart, going down the drain. Betrayed. Destroyed. Yet every generation testifies anew with its eyes and ears to what has been happening ever since the days of John the Baptist in Jerusalem, Galilee, Samaria and as far as the ends of the earth. How can we ever be truly free if we do not find our Lord and regard this as our supreme happiness? Too many Ralphs in the world don't want to take the risk of finding the Lord Jesus.

Rachel came bounding out of the monastery chapel and grabbed my coat. "Hey, Sister Gus, don't run off. Some of the guys have gone to find Father Richard and Brother

115

Dennis. We're going to have a quickie prayer meeting in the monastery parlor. A sort of send-off before we go off to practice. You're coming, too, aren't you?"

"Now that I know about it, you bet. How is the practice going, Rachel? I hear all kinds of rumors."

"Some of it has been strictly bad news, Sister Gus. Several of us were having a prayer meeting backstage—quiet like, you know. We just wanted to rejoice in the Lord and we weren't due on stage for a while. Well, one of the friars caught us and he blew a fuse. Wow, was he mad!"

"Why would he be mad if you were having a quiet prayer meeting?"

"He said that we should know better. We should know that prayer meetings weren't permitted at the school. Then he raked Brother Dennis over the coals for letting us do it during the practice. Really a bad scene."

We had reached the monastery parlor. Twelve of us. This was the third time I had come together with a group in this parlor that numbered twelve. Each of the two previous times had been exciting and quite unpredictable. I sensed this Sunday morning was going to be exciting, too.

One young man in particular caught my eye. He seemed to dance as he walked and was so animated. He was introduced as Kurt, the lad who played Mr. Appleby in *Damn Yankees*—Satan himself! Sylvia was off in a corner as though trying to decide whether to stay or go. There was a great deal of teasing and scuffling until Father Richard said very gently, "Shall we begin?"

Silence. Wonderful, pregnant, expectant silence. We sang and prayed and rejoiced. Then I heard Kurt speak, "Something's happening to me, man. I've never felt like this before. Man, I'm on fire. I just want to shout and praise the Lord."

116

And that's precisely what he did. He praised the Lord in a new language. The beauty of his prayer was magnified by another voice. Sylvia. Clear and bright and in perfect harmony. Arkie reached over to embrace Kurt and nearly smothered him. Rachel was squealing and hugging Sylvia. Cullen kept saying, "Thank You, Jesus" over and over. Bo was quiet but oh, such a radiance about his face. Tears were streaming down Molly's cheeks. Mitch smiled, wider and wider and wider.

When we had simmered down a bit, Father Richard's voice captured our attention as he prayed, "Father, thank You for Your Son. Thank You for Your Spirit. Thank You for the gifts we have witnessed here this morning. We lift these young people up to You and ask You to bless them. Lead them in a closer walk with Your Son, Jesus, Who loves them. We praise You and thank You for manifesting Your power in such a tangible way. Praise Jesus!"

Brother Dennis clapped Kurt on the back. "What a Satan you're going to be, now that you've got the baptism of the Spirit!"

Kurt seemed numb and happy. "I'll be an even better Satan than ever before. Wait and see!"

Sylvia's cheeks were still moist with tears as she came up beside me and said quietly, "I've found my hero, Sister Gus. I've found Him. Jesus. I didn't know it could be so wonderful."

As I hugged Sylvia I whispered, "This is only the beginning of your adventure, Syl. Every day brings new surprises and new wonders when we walk with Jesus." Whatever fragrance she was wearing, her black hair smelled like a field of wild flowers. So right for this vivacious young woman.

"Brother Dennis, won't we have a super practice to-

117

day?" observed Phyllis. "Just the best, I know. Wheeeeeeeeeeee!"

"You kids are going to have to put the damper on," cautioned Father Richard. "They're really watching you now."

"Let them watch," Arkie chirped. "We might convert a few of them, too."

The kids were leaving the Monastery parlor and heading for the scheduled practice as I commented to Father Richard, "Richard, you know you can't put the damper on the Holy Spirit! Especially not with these young people."

"I know," he answered wearily. "But I don't want them to get hurt any more than they have been for doing what should be every Christian's right—the right to pray."

"Jesus had to cope with the same kind of doubt and suspicion, so I don't guess we should be surprised when it happens to us and to the kids."

"I don't understand how they can justify that kind of attitude in a Catholic school."

"That seems to be the point, Richard. It's Catholic but not Christian."

"I wish there were some way I could convince my fellow Franciscans that this prayer is for real. It won't go away just because they come up with a new list of restrictions."

"Let the Holy Spirit do it! Want to come to the practice?"

"I can't today. Bo wants to talk to me. This seems to be one of his down times and it may take a while. Maybe next time."

As I pulled out of the monastery parking lot, I thought back on the events of this Sunday morning. Rachel was so right when she said "wow." It was strictly a wow ex-

118

perience from get-up time when the morning juices first started to circulate until now, just past high noon.

I found myself thinking about what paradise will be like when we'll be continually praising the Lord just as we were this morning. I can really get excited thinking about eternity. And so the speedometer indicated. I was doing 65 in a 45-mile-zone on Spring Grove Avenue.

"Slow down, Old Shoe," I told myself. "When the Lord is ready for you to enter the Promised Land, He'll arrange it."

He had arranged some wonderful events this morning. Who could say what the rest of the day would bring?

10. Glow, Baby, Glow

Down through the centuries, the theater has lured many to accept her as a way of life—mysterious, creative, enticing, demanding. Through the years I had dabbled in various Little Theater groups as performer and playwright. The glamour of the theater never seemed to diminish for me. My maternal grandmother had been with the theater in Austria before she married. Her family had ostracized her because "nice girls don't have anything to do with the stage." But grandmother followed the yearning of her heart and never returned to her native village. I'm sure I have some of her love of the theater flowing in my veins, too.

The stage at Roger Bacon High School was bare of props as the cast milled about waiting for practice to begin. Even in its barrenness, there was an air of excitement just being near a stage. So many had stood before those footlights.

Kurt jumped down off the stage and walked toward me. Rather, he danced toward me. "You'll have to really pray for me today, Sister Gus. I'll never get through those lines."

"I didn't realize you have trouble memorizing lines, Kurt."

"Ah, that's not what I mean. Sure, I know my lines. I did after the second practice. But how am I going to make like the devil himself when I'm feeling so good inside?"

"Perhaps you're about to create a new role—a *nice* Devil!"

"From what I've heard, the devil is always nice. That's how he traps us," Kurt stated emphatically.

"You'll have to step out of your new Spirit-filled self, Kurt, and let your voice be nasty. You've got to sneer and make them like it. But *only* while you're Mr. Appleby!"

"I can't believe what happened to me back there at the Monastery. It's like a super wonderful dream and I'm afraid I'll wake up and find out it was in my imagination."

"Kurt, it's real! And it is lasting if you want it to be. There's nothing magic about what happened to you. The Lord pure and simply gave you some powerful gifts. Use them for His glory and you'll grow and grow."

Our sharing session was abruptly ended as Mitch yelled from onstage, "Hey, Kurt, get your fanny up here. We're ready to roll."

Kurt bolted off toward the stage smiling much too much to be a convincing devil!

Damn Yankees was spritely and the kids were lively, though this was still a practice session. Looking at their faces, particularly in the chorus numbers, it wasn't difficult to pick out the Spirit-filled guys and gals. Or was it because I knew which ones were walking a deeper life in the Spirit? No. Definitely no. There *was* a distinct glow about them that made their whole person stand out in a line up. They were different. Wonderfully, glowingly different. Praise God!

The appearance of Lola onstage carried me back years into the past. It had taken me a long time to learn that I was never meant to be a Lola. Painful years until I realized I couldn't be anyone but myself. My own bap-

121

tism in the Spirit had been the crowning event in these years of discovery.

Kurt was magnificent as Mr. Appleby—cunning, teasing, placating, shrewd. A whole panorama of devices to which we have all succumbed along life's way. He *was* a nice devil. Nice and nasty! Like the real one who is so much alive and roaming about the world today. Have you ever noticed the uncomfortable facial expressions when you speak about the devil in any serious way? Your listeners want to turn you off right away. It's most disconcerting to admit that the devil is alive and among us. So much easier to pretend he just doesn't exist.

Brother Dennis appeared to be in another world at the piano. He had music in every cell. Because he loved music and enjoyed it, his enthusiasm was contagious. Opening night would probably make the fourth of July seem tame in comparison if even practice sessions were this incredibly scintillating.

Of all the charming songs of that sparkling production, the one that stuck in my brain all the way back to the convent was Lola's solo. "Whatever Lola wants, Lola gets—"

That song didn't apply to only the female of the species. Some men operated under that premise, too. I found myself thinking of Bart Newcomb. He hadn't been in touch since the prayer meeting he had attended. I hoped he had seen his physician. And I prayed often that he would let the Divine Physician really heal him!

I was jarred out of my reverie by the persistent honking of a Volkswagen that had pulled beside me in the passing zone. It sounded like the bleating of a sick lamb. In the dusk it took me a few moments before I recognized the driver of the other car. It was Jonathan and he was motioning me over to the curb.

When I came to an empty curb space I pulled in and

Jonathan zoomed his bug in behind me. Jonathan always looked like an unmade bed. His slight frame made him appear even younger than his eighteen years. And he had lived several lifetimes in those eighteen years.

I first met Jonathan on a boys' TEC. He captured my attention because he looked and moved like a person on drugs. He was. You name the vice, he had tried them all—several times. Though his physical appearance belied the fact, Jonathan had a magnetic personality and he dragged others with him on the road to iniquity and despair. Each time he hit bottom, he'd find his way back home somehow, often in the company of police officers. And each time his parents welcomed him home and tried desperately to understand what was driving their son to ruin.

Jonathan made that boys' TEC in a fog. There were hard battles for him, not mere skirmishes. As he explained it later, "I felt as though I were in the bottom of a garbage can, which is where I belonged. And nobody would be able to get me out. Then Father Rick started talking about how Jesus loves us no matter what we've done. It was then it hit me that Father Rick wasn't just talking to all the other guys; he was talking to me, too. I was included when he said that he was proclaiming the good news: 'you are forgiven.' Washed in the blood of the lamb. For the first time in my whole life, I felt clean. Clean, man, *clean!* Unless you've been really soiled by sin, you can't appreciate that feeling of being clean at last!"

Jonathan always reminded me of one of those mission ads for malnourished children. As he bounded toward my car, his slim frame brought that to mind again.

"Hey, Gus," Jonathan exploded. "This will blow your mind. Just had to tell you. Couldn't wait until the prayer meeting."

123

I'd cranked down the car window and was looking up into the lean face of Jonathan. "Lord," I thought, "You'd better put some meat on this one's bones or he'll blow away."

"Gus, this is out of sight. Just out of sight. I sat beside this chick at MacDonald's. I was with the guys and I didn't pay too much attention until I heard her sniffling. She was crying—but then dames are always crying. You know what I mean."

"They're not always crying, Jonathan, and you know it. But tell me about your new friend."

"Friend? Yeah, that's right. She's my friend now— now that I've told her about Jesus. You wouldn't believe her story, Gus. It sounds like a script for an X-rated movie. She had no place to go and no friends. Some joker dumped her off in Cincy because she couldn't stand the creep and didn't want to go the whole way with him. She really had nobody."

"Does she need a place to sleep, Jonathan? She could come home with me."

"Thanks, Gus, but the Lord took care of it another way. When I heard her sniffling, I asked if I could help. She couldn't talk just then so I started to witness to her what the Lord had done for me when I had hit absolutely rock bottom. She looks at me with those baby-blue eyes and says, 'But He doesn't care about me.' That really cracked me up. Because I've already been there when I thought He didn't care about me either. So I just talked to her quietly about Jesus and how He loves us no matter where we've been or what we've been up to. She had stopped crying by then. Gee, Gus, she was the prettiest thing."

"So what did you do then to help the little lady?"

"I told her the truth. I told her if she gave her life to Jesus He would take care of all her problems. I could

124

tell it was a real struggle for her. I don't know much about this demonology stuff or whatever you call it but I felt there was an awful force working against me. So I remembered what we did at the prayer meeting and I bound the evil spirit in prayer. Then this chick—her name is Lily—simmered down and she says, 'I really want to believe what you say. I want to give my life to Jesus. But I'm scared.' She was, too. She was trembling."

An irate driver honked at us though we weren't blocking traffic. His lane was free for him to zoom on up Colerain Avenue. Maybe it had been a hard day for him.

Jonathan continued, "Lily looked at me through her tears and said she wanted to give her life to Jesus. She wanted to give it a try. We started to pray over her right there in MacDonald's and out of the blue, Sara Kate walked in. I know now it really wasn't 'out of the blue.' The Lord had planned it the whole time. We told Sara Kate about Lily and before very long, Sara Kate was inviting Lily to come home with her and stay until she found herself a job and a place to live in Cincy. Hey, Gus, isn't Jesus something else?"

"Oh, yes, Jonathan!" I had goosebumps, inverted ones, all over! "He's something else. If Lily needs any clothes, let me know. Otherwise, I'll see you at Toby's baptism tomorrow."

As quickly as he had zoomed his bug into the curb, just as rapidly Jonathan moved out again into the mainstream of traffic before I even had my Dodge Dart cranked up. It was such a joy to see him sparkling and alive. Such a contrast to the mesmerized Jonathan who was tripping all during the boys' TEC.

This would be no ordinary baptism. It was Pentecost Sunday, May 14, 1972, and I was gift-wrapping my special gift for Toby. This was the day he was to be baptized. And, we hoped, the day he would also receive the baptism of the Holy Spirit in its fullness.

Toby was a beautiful example of one who had been clay in the hands of the Master Potter, Jesus. From the first time he had appeared at one of our prayer meetings, apprehensive and shy, he had grown to the magnificent stature of one fully given to the Lord and His work. As the weeks had evolved, Toby had felt an increasing compulsion to give himself fully to the Lord. He had been attending Catholic school and knew the doctrine. Now he knew the person of Jesus and he wanted to be His man all the way. Through instruction and discussion with Father Richard, Toby had come to the conclusion that he wanted to become a Catholic. His parents attended a classical Pentecostal church. They felt Toby was old enough to make this decision for himself.

The kids decided they would plan the ceremony, and they did it with a flourish. They were so excited and pleased to be part of this very important occasion in the life of our prayer community. Chesty was to be Toby's godfather. And serene, prayerful Carrie was to be his godmother. The ceremony would be in the monastery chapel and an open invitation was extended to our prayer community and to the Community of Hope.

Pentecost dawned bright and sunny. I was so anxious for the hours to flit by, so that the time of the afternoon ceremony would come round quickly. But it didn't. At the convent we had guests and I couldn't get away until after 2 P.M. I'd be late. But at least I would get there.

When I arrived at the monastery, the chapel was packed, including the sanctuary. Toby was standing before the altar with Father Richard and I was especially attracted to the "Holy Spirit" candle designed for the occasion. It was in the shape of a huge white dove with seven wicks.

Such a glow! But nothing to compare with the glow on Toby's face.

As I entered, Brother Dennis was singing a hymn to the Holy Spirit written by a monk from the Abbey of Gethsemane. So many of the kids from our prayer meeting had come plus a goodly number from the Community of Hope—including some of the fiercest skeptics from the group. They weren't missing a thing.

As the part of the ceremony came when the person seeking baptism usually recites the Creed, Father Richard turned to Toby and said, "Toby, will you tell us in your own words why you want to be baptized a Christian."

The monastery chapel was deafeningly quiet as Toby began to express his reasons. No theologian could have done better. At the conclusion, he turned toward his parents and said, "In case you're wondering what's happened to your boy, well, I've just found Jesus!"

There is a point in the baptismal ceremony when the priest puts on the catechumen, the white robe of baptism. The kids had decided that Toby would look like an overgrown altar boy if they stuck a white surplice on him so his godmother, Carrie, made him a white dashiki with a floral trim at the neck and wrist. Such a fitting robe for a black man being baptized!

As Father Richard poured the water over Toby's forehead and intoned those words ever ancient and ever new, "I baptize you in the name of the Father and of the Son and of the Holy Spirit" I was mentally making an addition. "Do baptize Toby, Lord Jesus, with the fire and power of your Holy Spirit. Complete his baptism in its fullness today. We ask this in Your all powerful name, Jesus, and we thank You because You have heard our prayer."

I know I didn't really have to pray that prayer, because

so many of the kids had already prayed it in the days before the baptism ceremony. But those words just had to come out at that moment. One of the usual chaotic Kiss-of-Peace movements began at that instant and I was swept along by the rest.

Cameras were clicking; flashbulbs were popping. Such a melee—and yet it was thrillingly joyful and so perfect for the occasion. In the back of the church I noticed one couple unabashedly smooching. There were some stone faces who obviously objected to the outburst. Toby was ecstatic. Chesty was flying high and Carrie was deliriously happy. Toby's parents were quiet, probably mystified by some of the activities. But they seemed genuinely pleased that their son had accepted Jesus as Lord of his life.

The kids had presented Toby with a handsome edition of the *Jerusalem Bible* as their gift to him. I had made him a colorful banner using the quote from Song of Songs 2:5, "His banner over me is love." Toby was special to all of us.

I think Brother Dennis pulled out all the stops on the Monastery organ as he began to play "Amazing Grace." Such volume. And our voices matched it. Deafening and magnificent.

Toby was engulfed by the kids. People were milling everywhere. Some were still singing "Praise God" long after the organ had ceased. Several of us had agreed that we wanted to have a quiet prayer meeting after the baptism to praise God for the day. I was making my way up through the chapel crowd to the sanctuary when I was confronted head-on by Nick.

Nick was a fiery Italian with cold, black eyes that reminded me of ripe olives. He was a member of the Community of Hope and was always giving our kids a lot of static because of their witnessing. He referred to them as "Jesus creeps" and was the last person I would have expected to see at this baptism.

"Well, Sister," Nick snarled, "you roped another one in, didn't you?"

There's no point in arguing with a man of such an unbending attitude. I smiled and greeted Nick with a half-way pleasant "Good afternoon, Nick. Is your family with you?"

Nick had many children, ten or twelve, and a quiet, mousey wife. Nick felt he was invincible. Every sermon at every Mass he picked apart. Then he picked the personality of the celebrant apart. On one particular Sunday during Lent, at coffee and doughnuts time after Mass, Nick seemed to wait until a group was gathered around and then blurted out, directing his remarks at me, "That boy priest friend of yours really got wound up at Mass this morning, didn't he? What a bunch of—"

"If you find Father Richard's sermons so offensive, why do you come?" I asked.

"I keep hoping he'll wake up from his dream world and get some sense," Nick continued. "These young punks just out of the seminary think they got all the answers and that the rest of us are a bunch of meatheads."

Sam was standing beside me and intervened. "Father Richard was simply preaching a Christian message this morning, straight from the Bible. You'll find it all in First Corinthians."

Nick didn't have a chance to continue his snide remarks because the coffee and doughnuts line crowded us apart. Thank God! I have prayed much for him and his family and by the expression in his face as he looked at me this Pentecost afternoon, I knew he still needed prayer very much.

Those black eyes of Nick's were brimming with a desperate loneliness and emptiness. They reminded me of

Sara Kate's eyes when she had first spoken of witchcraft. In my heart I was praying that Jesus would bind whatever evil spirits were holding Nick in bondage. He seemed about to speak but no words were audible.

"Jesus, give me the words to say to this man—*now!*"

And Jesus heard my plea. With a mighty anointing I found myself talking to a man I couldn't tolerate under ordinary conditions. But these were not ordinary conditions. By his uncommon silence, Nick was speaking volumes to me, and he was hurting—bad.

"Nick, don't you know that Jesus really loves you just as He loves everyone else here? You've seen His love exteriorized in so many ways this past hour here at this baptism. You aren't here by accident, you know. Jesus planned for you to be here today so that you, too, might be washed with living water and be made a new man. Just as Toby was, right here before your eyes. This is where it's at, Nick. Right here in the love Christians have for one another because they are united to one head—Jesus."

During the baptism I had been thinking that the Lord would surely manifest His power today, Pentecost. And now I was seeing that power operative right before my eyes. A single tear was rolling down each cheek of Nick's swarthy face. He still didn't speak.

"Nick, it's all so simple and it's for you. Just turn over your life completely to Jesus. Stop fighting it. Hang loose. And you'll be a new man."

Then an unexpected thing happened. I felt the presence of evil so strongly as Nick's black eyes now burned with fury. He seemed to be drooling and his mouth was twitching. He shoved me against the pew and spat out the words, "You God damned—" and his words trailed off but I could guess their content. Pushing his way back through the chapel, Nick literally plunged out the door and toward the parking lot.

I stood motionless and weak in the knees. It was almost as if I had seen the devil sitting on Nick's shoulder, he was so real. Slowly I groped my way toward the small prayer group. I needed the sustaining power of their prayer at that moment. The woman in me wanted to weep, loud and long. But I glanced over at Toby and only tears of joy came. I couldn't look at that happy face and be sad.

"Jesus, Nick is Your baby. Please rescue him from his own self-destruction. Don't let him be lost. He needs You so badly." No more words would come. The Spirit would supply the rest!

But I was not to have the luxury of quiet prayer at this time. Brother Mark sat beside me and whispered, "There's a policeman in the monastery parlor who wants to see you."

A zillion thoughts raced through my brain on my way to the monastery parlor. Was one of the kids in trouble? On drugs again? Hurt? Lost? Suicide? Is it ever possible to think a happy thought when you're summoned by a policeman? Must it always be bad news?

The police officer was in his mid-forties, I guessed. The name on his uniform was "Cirillo." He was friendly and appeared to have a bit of Irish mixed in with the Italian heritage suggested by his name.

"Sister Augustine, I'm Officer Cirillo of the Cincinnati Police Force and I've just come from the emergency room of Good Samaritan Hospital."

My hands were icy yet I was perspiring waiting for the inevitable bad news.

He continued, "We just brought a girl to Good Sam, unconcious. She doesn't have any identification but she did have a book in her coat pocket that has your address label in it. We called your convent and they told us we'd find you here. Could you come with us and identify the girl?"

"What does she look like, Officer?"

"When she isn't all messed up like she is now, she's probably a good-looking dame. Probably in her early twenties, I'd say. Long blond hair, bleached. Slim. Curves in the right places. Too much make-up. Think you know who that might be, Sister?"

I looked at Brother Mark and we knew simultaneously who it was—Mimi! Poor, desperate, struggling Mimi!

"Officer, what did you mean when you said she was 'messed up'?"

"Somebody really worked her over, Sister, before they left her in that alley where we found her. But she's still breathing."

"Let me get my Bible, Officer, and I'll come with you at once."

I was numb as I sat in the front seat of Patrol Car Number 66 zooming down Colerain Avenue. There wasn't too much traffic that Sunday afternoon. For those who were on the road, I couldn't blame them for staring at this incongruous pair—a police officer and a nun in the front seat of a patrol car in Cincinnati.

I tried to pray but the whole situation seemed incomprehensible to me. "Jesus, how could You let this happen on Pentecost of all days? Don't You remember that I asked You for a great outpouring of Your Spirit today?"

Like the wail of the siren it hit me: I am giving you a great outpouring of My Spirit, the Lord seemed to be telling me. Just get out of the way and let it work to My glory!

I felt the Lord's presence strongly as I entered the Emergency Ward. The nurse in me felt right at home in such surroundings. But even the nurse in me wasn't prepared for the battered body of Mimi. Hot tears burned

132

my eyes and I clenched my fists so hard my fingernails dug into my palms. Who could have done such a thing?

"Can you identify her, Sister?" Officer Cirillo was asking in a very businesslike way.

"Yes, I can identify her as far as her first name is concerned. Her name is Mimi. That's all I know."

"She evidently doesn't have any next of kin."

"You can list me as her next of kin, Officer. Right now I think I'm all the family she's got."

Officer Cirillo looked at me dubiously, but he wrote my name and address in the "next of kin" slot. When I told him I planned to stay with Mimi and he didn't have to worry about getting me back to the monastery to my car, he seemed even more puzzled.

"Sister, you don't have to stay. There's no obligation. I just needed somebody to identify her."

"I'm glad to stay, Officer. Thank you for coming to get me."

He was shaking his head as he walked away. I stepped away from the table so that the resident physician and nurse could care for Mimi. Where on that bruised body could they start?

"You start, Jesus," I prayed. "Start with her heart. Heal Mimi's heart first so that she'll know how much You love her and how much we love her. Heal every cell in her body so that she will be whole again. I lift up to You in prayer the persons who did this terrible thing to her. They need Your help, Jesus. Bless them and help them find their way to You."

Then I heard it. The sound like a wounded animal whimpering. It was Mimi, too weak to make any great sound but definitely in pain. I moved closer to the table while the resident automatically started an I.V. Mimi's face was distorted in pain. The nurse was giving her an

133

injection—so efficient and so sterile. I leaned toward Mimi and called her name.

Through her mental fog, the words came so slowly, "Gus—don't let them hurt me any more—"

"No one's going to hurt you, Mimi," I consoled. "You're in the hospital. I'll be right here with you. Let the medicine do its work and the pain will ease. Then you can get some rest. And when you wake up and are feeling stronger, we can talk some more. We all care about you, Mimi."

Tears were rolling down her swollen face. Perhaps from pain, perhaps from a great release. The nurse informed me very crisply that they would be taking Mimi to X-Ray before she was put in a hospital bed. As I walked beside the cart carrying Mimi's still form I thought of Officer Cirillo's comment, "She evidently doesn't have any next of kin."

"Oh, yes, she does," I thought. "All of us in the prayer group are going to be her next of kin. She will have a numberless family all ready to receive her and make her one of us—if she wants it that way. Please, Lord Jesus, let it be so. Let us be Mimi's family."

11. Lonesome Everywhere

The 12th chapter of 1 Corinthians came alive for me during the weeks of Mimi's hospitalization. The kids took their body ministry seriously. Their concern for Mimi was sincere, yet many of them had not actually met her. Some, on their own, decided to fast especially for Mimi's recovery. All manner of thoughtful gestures were evidenced in the many cards and flowers she received. Chesty was a daily visitor though he hadn't dated Mimi in a while.

> God has arranged the body so that more dignity is given to the parts which are without it, and so that there may not be disagreements inside the body, but that each part may be equally concerned for all the others. If one part is hurt, all parts are hurt with it. [1 Corinthians 12:24-26]

Through all of this, I could see the kids growing in a deeper walk with the Lord. It's one thing to read about such crimes on the front page of the local newspaper and then blot it from your mind; but it's quite another to be involved with the person who has been victim of a brutal crime. Frequently I prayed that the Lord would heal Mimi's memory so that the awful event would be erased and she could be at peace.

Mimi is a fighter and in this time of her life, that was an advantage. She had internal bleeding and the doctor considered doing an exploratory laparotomy but her vital signs were too poor to risk it. Blood transfusions helped. Prayers were answered and the surgery wasn't necessary. The bleeding subsided.

On one of my visits to the hospital, I met Officer Cirillo. He was in civilian clothes this time and didn't look so officious.

"Sister, we need your cooperation in this case involving Mimi."

I had visions of having to appear in court in some lengthy legal hassle and groaned inwardly as Officer Cirillo continued.

"We think we know who the guys were who beat up on Mimi but she won't give us any information to confirm it. And we can't prosecute unless we have some identification. Could you help us get the information from her?"

"Maybe she doesn't know any more than she's told you."

"Sister, I work with this kind of broad all the time. They know plenty—for a price."

"Why do you think these men would have beaten Mimi? Or is that information classified?"

"No, it's not classified. It's the usual. On the side, Mimi is a pusher. The guys wanted the stuff and she wouldn't give it up without the money. You probably didn't think she was that kind of girl when you gave her that book we found in her coat pocket."

How can you explain to a man like this what you really know about a girl like Mimi—about her pain and hurt and rejection that drove her to prostitution and dope pushing? I had given her a copy of Sammy Hall's *Hooked on a Good Thing* precisely because I knew she

136

was hooked on a bad thing. I wondered if she had even cracked the cover of the book.

"Officer, I can't guarantee that Mimi would confide in me. She's not too fond of nuns. But if I do collect any information, I'll bring it to your attention. That's as much as I can promise."

"We'll be grateful. Our work gets so frustrating when the very people who have been molested won't cooperate in giving us needed information. Thanks for your help, Sister," he concluded as he walked toward the elevator.

My visits to Mimi had been strained, but I understood her reticence. She had made it clear from our first meeting that she wasn't interested in communicating with me. So my stay with her each time was brief. At least she would know that I cared about her.

Propped up in her hospital bed, wearing a frilly gown with her hair pulled back in braids, Mimi looked like an advertisement for Miss Teenage America. Until you noticed the dark circles under her wide eyes and the hard lines around her mouth. The dark roots of her hair were showing and this made her appearance even more severe.

Slowly she graduated from bed to arm chair and then ambulation. But she never seemed to smile. Even when the kids would come to visit, Mimi was very solemn. She had flatly refused to discuss the incident of Pentecost Sunday that brought her to the hospital. Officer Cirillo would have to get his information from another source.

Three weeks after Pentecost when I went to the hospital, I found a much older woman in the bed Mimi had occupied. I assumed she had been moved to another bed. When I inquired at the nurses' desk, I was informed that Mimi had been discharged.

"That's impossible," was my reaction. "When?"

"About noon today," the nurse answered. "The doctor felt Miss Reynolds could convalesce at home."

It sounded so strange to hear Mimi referred to as "Miss Reynolds."

"But she doesn't have a home."

"She must have made some sort of arrangements," the nurse commented in a proficient manner. "A young man came to call for her and brought her clothes."

I'm sure my mouth was hanging open. I didn't think Mimi was strong enough to leave the hospital for unknown surroundings. Under my breath I was offering a rather choice blessing for the doctor who signed her out of the hospital.

Walking down the hospital corridor, I reminded Jesus of a prayer I had uttered for Mimi before. "She's in Your hands, Jesus. Take care of her wherever she is right now."

In such deep thought, I nearly collided with a young man carrying a tray of sterile supplies. It was Sam. He looked so different in his hospital white.

"Sam, what are you doing here? You look like you're part of the furnishings."

"I am," Sam beamed. "I've been working here as an orderly since last month. That's why I've had to miss some of the prayer meetings. But I need the money for tuition. And I like it. Gives me lots of chances to witness."

"One look at you would be witness enough," I observed. "You're beaming. The best medicine ever for sick folks!"

"Yeah, that's what I figure, Sister Gus. Some of the guys thought I'd freaked out when they heard I was working as an orderly. But I really felt led by the Lord to apply. I put out a little Gideon's fleece. You know what I mean. If the Lord wanted me here, I'd get the job; if He didn't, then they wouldn't hire me. Right?"

138

"Right," I answered beaming back at Sam. You had to respond. His smile was contagious.

"I'm headed for my coffee break, Sister Gus. Do you have time to join me? That will really blow their minds, if they see me walking in with a nun!"

"I'd like to be your guest, Sam. That is, if you don't think it will be too much of a shock for your fellow workers," I teased.

"By this time of day, they can probably use a jolt," Sam commented as we walked into the snack bar. Several other orderlies greeted Sam. There seemed to be a good spirit among them.

Sam captured an empty booth. I admired this young man very much. He'd gotten to the heart of the Christian message so quickly at a time when most collegians are offering all kinds of intellectual and philosophical arguments against God.

"What's the Lord been doing in your life lately, Sam?"

Sam stared down into his coffee cup for a few moments before he answered. "Really weird lately, Sister Gus. Weird. You know what that Jesus did? Well, what's happening is that I'm one of those guys who are almost constantly being whacked with all sorts of big old hairy doubts about the Lord and all sorts of things like that. I guess some of the stuff I get in class brings it on."

"Can you handle it?"

"You know how it goes. Some people get an overdose when it comes to the gift of faith, and me—well— So what I did is I started praying for greater and stronger faith, you know. Like you had told us once that you asked the Lord to baptize you with fire and He took you at your word. Remember that?"

"Oh, yes, I remember."

"I think there must be a difference in the kind of faith I mean when I ask for a super dose and the kind of faith

139

the Lord means. *I* meant the kind of faith that would make it really easy to believe, and that nothing could shake my faith in Jesus. Well, what *He* seems to have meant is that no matter what kind of doubts I have—I'll still hang on, in spite of everything. I think that's kinda sneaky."

"Sneaky? Sam, the Lord is paying you the highest kind of compliment to trust you enough to put you in a few storms. The storms make us stronger."

"I guess my faith is getting stronger. Anymore when those stupid doubts (actually, some of them seem rather intelligent, but they're still stupid!) come along, I just say, 'I don't care. You can bug me all you want but I'm still gonna believe in Jesus as Lord!' And those doubts are the kind that would have blown me away a few months ago. Praise the Lord! Sister Gus, we sure do have a neat God. I really dig Him."

Sam was delightfully different from the usual college junior. I found his casual manner when speaking of God wonderfully refreshing. Interlaced with his own special vernacular, conversation with Sam was a joy.

"Hey, I've gotta run. Sure nice to have talked with you, Sister Gus. Tell Father Rick I haven't dropped out of sight. Just goofy hours in a hospital." And off he went to bring cheer to some bedridden soul.

I checked my watch and realized I'd have to hurry to be on time for my appointment with Father Richard at the Monastery. Neither of us wanted to make business appointments for Sunday, but the matter was urgent and there never seemed to be enough time in a weekday schedule. We had planned to discuss the matter of Julie, "sweet Julie" as I called her.

Julie had made the last girls' TEC. Always wide-eyed, her face looked like a perpetual exclamation point. She was a charming young lady, seventeen. During the TEC

140

retreat, I noticed that Julie didn't mix too well with the other girls. She seemed uncommonly quiet and moved slowly for one so young. When I gave part of my testimony during the retreat, the Lord had moved me to include the story of my nurse friend, Jo, who became pregnant to a married man, and how she handled the whole affair. Plus my own role in the saga.

During a quiet time following that conference, Julie had slumped into a chair beside me and softly asked, "Sister Gus, could you help another pregnant gal? Like me? Like right now?"

I didn't know anything about Julie except the name of her school. Judging from her clothes, money was evidently no problem. Those wide eyes burned into my brain as I tried to delicately choose the right words for this young woman.

"I'd like to help, Julie. But I need a little background."

"I should tell you right off that I'm not Catholic."

"That doesn't make any difference, Julie. I'd want to help even if you had no religion."

"I'm almost three months along. And neither the guy's folks or my folks want us to get married. They think they made that decision for us. But we made that decision ourselves, that we weren't going to get married. Just because we made a mistake is no reason to rush into a marriage. Don't you think so, Sister?"

"I agree that no one, whatever their age, should rush into marriage. It's a lifelong commitment. Have you made any plans about having the baby?"

Tears were spilling out of those wide eyes and Julie was finding it difficult to speak. I gathered her up in one bear hug and neither of us spoke for a time.

"Like I said, Sister, I'm not Catholic. But I still don't believe anybody can destroy a life. My folks want me to have an abortion. You know, go off to New York where no one would recognize me and have it done. I don't want to do that. Not in New York or any other place. I want to have the baby and put it up for adoption. I've read about plenty of people who want babies and can't have them. Somebody would adopt the baby. Do you know of any place I could go during the last few months when I start to really show? Some place where I could go until the baby comes?"

"Yes, I do know of such a place. But we would need your parents' permission."

Again the tears. "They won't consent, Sister. I'll have to sneak away somehow."

"Julie, suppose you let Father Richard and me see what arrangements we can make. We can go and talk with your parents."

"Please do something. Please help me." Her slim body was shaken with sobs as I tried to console her.

When Julie was quiet again, I asked her how she came to be on the retreat. "I just had to come," she answered. "The guy I did it with, you know; well, he made the last boys' TEC. I couldn't believe he was the same guy afterwards. He told me about the things Father Richard said about being forgiven, no matter what you've done, if you're sorry. And how Jesus loves us. I guess I couldn't believe anyone could love me as I am. So I had to come to hear it for myself. And he was right. It makes you all different inside when you realize what Father Richard says about Jesus is true. Then when you told us about your nurse friend, Jo, I knew this was the Lord's way of answering my prayer for help. You were the answer. You would help me. I'm glad I came on the retreat."

"I'm glad, too, Julie. I'm glad the Lord arranged it. We'll be going to the chapel now for prayer. Let's agree right here that we'll both lift this whole situation up to the Lord in prayer. He will show us the right way to go with this event in your life. You belong to Jesus. He's your answer, Julie."

Without another word, we walked toward the chapel. I felt such a compassion for Julie I didn't want to let her go. In the quiet, dim interior of the monastery chapel, I experienced such a deep peace. The presence of the Lord was overpowering as I commended sweet Julie to Him.

Now as I waited in the monastery parlor for Father Richard to appear, I tried to gather my thoughts concerning the options we had to help Julie. I felt strongly led to approach her parents as soon as possible.

Father Richard walked into the parlor as though he were carrying some heavy burden. There was no smile or greeting only the comment, "You just missed it."

"Missed what?" I asked, mystified.

"Julie's telephone call."

"Is she coming over?"

"She should be halfway to New York by now."

"New York? Richard, *no!* They're not making her go!"

"They are making her go. In fact, her parents are with her on this trip."

"They *can't* make her have an abortion," I literally screamed it. "They *can't.*"

"She's still a minor under her parents' roof. They do have the right to do what they're doing, horrendous as it seems."

I couldn't say another word. There was too much fury in me. I pictured sweet Julie, trapped and in agony. Sweet Julie who so loved life and living things she wouldn't even step on a bug. I couldn't pray. I couldn't think. I couldn't do anything except keep repeating her name—as though somehow that would permit me to make contact with this lovable young woman to help ease the trauma of what was about to happen. The impersonal probing and the yanking from her of a life that had just begun! No! Sweet Julie—sweet Julie—sweet Julie—

When words would come again and I had stopped blubbering, I turned toward Richard who looked as miserable as I sounded and asked him, "How did you find out about Julie's trip to New York?"

"Only minutes before you arrived, I was called to the phone. It was Julie calling from the airport. She was crying, hard. She said her folks were checking in at the airlines and she had slipped away to the nearest phone. The desperation in her voice was shattering. She kept saying over and over, 'Help me. Please help me. I don't want to go.' I still hear her."

"Oh, Richard, couldn't we try to make it to the airport before they take off? If it was that short a time ago, we might make it."

"No, I'm afraid we can't. In the middle of a sentence, I heard a man's voice—probably her father. He shouted at Julie, 'Come on. After all the trouble you've been, do you want us to miss the plane, too? Get off that phone!' She didn't even have a chance to say good-bye."

A sudden summer thunderstorm added to the gloom of our misery. The raindrops pelting against the windowpane reminded me of Julie's tears—and mine.

"My first reaction was the same as yours, Gus. I wanted to jump in the car and make a dash for the airport. I felt I had to be *doing* something visibly, tangibly to help Julie. But it was as though the Lord had put a restraining hand on me and was telling me to cool it. That Julie is in His hands no matter how cruel and inhuman this whole mess seems to us right at this moment. And then my bell rang and Brother Mark told me you were here."

With the rainstorm for background, we joined hands and prayed—the powerful silent kind of prayer that ascends to the Lord from troubled hearts. I prayed for sweet Julie as I would my own sister if I had been blessed with one. I surely loved her as though she were my own flesh and blood. I prayed for her parents. There is no way to know what personal agonies they had suffered through all of this, too.

Crowding into my cranium were various images of what the abortion clinic must be like—the kind of people who must staff it—the pictures I'd seen of fetuses thrown in a garbage can—slimy, dirty, ugly images. It was so real to me I was soaked with perspiration and violently sick. I made a dash for the bathroom as Father Richard stared in amazement. I knew what he must be thinking: "Woman! The eternal enigma!"

After the worst of my physical storm, I came back into the parlor and noted the summer thunderstorm had ceased, too. Father Richard and I decided to walk outdoors as we continued our discussion. A moist greeting from Jenny, the monastery's affectionate St. Bernard dog, brought me to reality.

"Richard, I keep trying to think of what we can do when Julie gets back here. She *is* coming back to Cincinnati, isn't she?"

"As far as I know, she will. This clinic is advertised as a weekend deal so they must have speedy service," Richard commented acidly.

"I wish Julie would come to the prayer meetings so she could feel the support of the praying community. But I wonder what restrictions her parents may put on her when they return."

"Though I'm sure this abortion thing is a traumatic experience for any woman, I think it must be even more so for someone like Julie who didn't want it. Let's keep claiming her healing—the healing of her memories," Father Richard suggested.

145

"Maybe we could get the word around to some of our key people in the prayer meeting for them to be on an extra alert for Julie and follow His leading on how we can best help her mend—totally."

"Right," Richard agreed as we neared the parking lot. "Are you going back to the convent from here?"

"Not just yet. I'm going to drive over to Mount Airy forest, find me a quiet spot under a tree, and get myself glued back together. Then maybe I can go back to the convent and face my community."

I meant to turn and get into the car. Instead, I turned facing Richard and blurted out, "Richard, where did we go wrong in all this mess with Julie?"

Calmly and peacefully, he replied. "We didn't go wrong. We just have to know that there are some events in life over which we have no control. But if we really trust in the Lord, we can know with certainty that this whole mess *is* in His hands and in ways unknown to us, He will bring good from it. Wait on the Lord, Gus. He won't let Julie be lost to us."

I wanted to reply but no words would come. I had no more tears. I was drained.

There are moments in life when words are utterly useless. This was one of them. But I knew Richard understood as wordlessly I waved goodbye and drove toward Mount Airy Forest. The words of the poet Shelley came to my mind: "Silence is also conversation." And what volumes had just been spoken in the last few minutes!

12. In Reverse

The man walking in front of me down Vine Street had the swagger of Bart Newcomb but he seemed too stooped over, too old, too slow to be Bart. I hadn't seen him since that prayer meeting at O.L.A. When the man in front of me had to stop to wait for the traffic signal to change, I caught up with him. We stared at each other almost in embarrassment. He *was* Bart Newcomb!

In a draggy monotone, Bart greeted me with "Hi, Gus." He'd lost weight. There were dark circles under his eyes. Respirations too rapid.

"Hi, Bart. Seems ages since I last talked with you. What's been happening?"

"The usual. Had a spell in bed. Flu, I guess. I've been meaning to get in touch again. Carla's been giving me a rough time. My real estate business is collapsing right in front of my eyes. Everything's going wrong, Gus."

Bart's voice conveyed his frustration and agitation. His eyes, usually sharp and flinty, were drab and listless.

"Let's find a quiet place to talk, Bart. The traffic sounds on this corner are deafening."

"Where are you going to find a place to talk on Vine Street? I know you won't go into one of these peep show joints."

"All these buildings aren't peep shows or adult book

147

stores on Vine Street. We can go to the Christian Book Store. Isabella has a nice quiet corner there."

"A Christian book store on Vine Street, Gus? You're going soft in the head. It must be a front for some other activity. Are you sure she's not a madam?"

"Quite sure." I chuckled to myself and wondered how many others who had come to the corner of Ninth and Vine streets had asked the same question. The Christian Book Store was an oasis in the midst of adult peep shows, go-go girls, prostitutes, pushers, winos. Name any vice the world has known, and you can find it on Vine Street. But like life itself, Vine Street isn't all bad.

As I opened the door of the Christian Book Store I was as enchanted by the mellow tinkling bells and warm, friendly surroundings as I had been on my first visit. Isabella called a cheery "Praise the Lord" and waved as Bart and I entered. I directed Bart back to the "prayer corner" as I had affectionately dubbed the rear area of the store. Isabella and I had shared many prayers, joys and troubles in that special corner. So had countless others.

Bart slumped into the nearest chair. I prayed for the guidance of the Spirit, a radar beacon to choose the right words to speak to my troubled friend and the right times to remain silent. Some of the Jesus people from C.I.C. were in the front of the store sharing a new song the Lord had given them with Isabella. It lifted my heart but Bart was oblivious to the melody or the lyrics. Wrapped up in himself and his woes, he was a portrait of dejection and self-pity.

"Gus, you wouldn't believe the mess I've gotten in since the last time you saw me. I was so sure Carla would go straight after that bad trip she had. But she hasn't. She's not on the stuff around the clock, understand, but I know she's still on it. It's that creep Jake. I told her to dump that guy but they seem more serious than ever." Bart slammed his fist into his palm to emphasize his concern.

"You know enough about the human condition to understand why Carla follows this behavior pattern, Bart."

"Confound it, Gus. Are you going to plop the blame for this in my lap again?" The flint was returning and that was a good sign!

Answering his own problems, Bart continued thoughtfully. "O.K. So Carla goes back on the stuff and hangs on to that boob Jake because she's protesting my separation from her mother—"

"Is that the only reason you see for her protest?" I asked.

Flint and fire were in command now. "If I want to live with some chick, that's my business. Not my kid's business! Understand?"

I understood. Completely. Bart's conscience was screaming for release. He was perspiring again just as he had at the prayer meeting when Father Richard had spoken of God's unlimited forgiveness.

In a softer tone, Bart commented, "Besides, that's not part of the picture any more. The dame left when I got sick. I haven't been with her for almost a month. Don't even know where she is right now."

"Does Carla realize you haven't been with her?"

"How would I know? I didn't plan to send out an all-points bulletin." More flint. Good!

"Bart, each of us has made whopping mistakes. The real tragedy is when we haven't learned from those mistakes."

"I'm too unglued to get into any philosophical discussion, Gus. Carla will find out in time without my telling her. What will hurt even more is when Marcia and the kids find out my business is a bust, too. For years I've watched other guys around me crumble financially because they got hung up on booze and dames. I vowed that would never happen to me. I'd know when to slow down. And I was 1000% wrong."

"Bart, why don't you start all over? You're still young as executives go. With your fierce determination, channeled in the right direction, you'll get your business out of the skids and back into the commercial arena in a short time."

The Jesus people had left the book store and the only sound was that of the traffic on Vine Street. Bart was bent forward and his ashen color concerned me.

"Before you do anything, Bart, promise me you'll see a good internist. Part of your defeatist attitude may very well be poor health."

"It was just the flu. Nothing more."

"Perhaps. But just to make certain you're completely rid of the bug, call for an appointment. Soon. Like right now. Isabella won't mind if you use her phone."

"I'm too tired to argue with you, Gus. You make it for me. With that doctor on Colerain you're always raving about. Let my secretary know when it is so she can remind me. I think I'll take a drive over to Calhoun Street to see if Carla and her roommate will have lunch with me."

And off he went. Walking a bit straighter with the military bearing I always associated with Bart. I made his doctor's appointment and then rested in the Lord for a time there in that special haven on the corner of Ninth and Vine.

Isabella was busy with customers as I prepared to leave. I called to her across the store, "Send me a bill for space rental."

"That will cost you five minutes worth of praising the Lord," Isabella replied. Her smile sent me on my way

with my heart lifted and my mind at peace about Bart
Newcomb.

Turning up Vine Street I was trying to walk at a brisk
pace so that I could catch the noon Mass at the Cathedral. A hulk of a young man bumped into me pushing
me against a bar front with his weight. He wasn't too
steady on his feet. Looking into his face, I realized he
was high on drugs. It was as though someone had kicked
me in the abdomen and knocked all the wind out of my
sails as I looked into his face—not the face of a stranger
but the face of Chesty. He looked at me with a "get out
of my way, babe" kind of expression devoid of any
recognition. I wanted to call out his name but my voice
froze. His buddy steered him into a narrow doorway
and they were gone. The press of the noon crowd propelled
me on up Vine Street.

I got to the Cathedral just as the lector was about to
read the day's epistle from Galatians 4. With Bart and
Chesty so present in my awareness, I welcomed those com-
forting words of Scripture. "Abba, Father," the epistle
said. "You are a son not a slave any more." Yes, they
are both God's sons and He will care for them.

The lector read on, "Now that God has acknowledged you, how can you want to go back to elemental
things like these, that can do nothing and give nothing,
and be their slaves?" I was wishing I could rush out into
the streets of Cincinnati and scoop up all the Barts and
Chestys and bring them here into the Cathedral where
there was such a benediction of peace. As the congrega-
tion prayed the responsorial psalm, the Spirit nudged my
memory. I thought of another verse from Galatians 4
that has loomed into my life so often and here it was
again like a blazing neon sign: "I must go through the
pain of giving birth to you all over again, until Christ
is formed in you." (Galatians 4:19).

151

"Yes, Lord," I prayed. "I will have to go through the birth pains again for Chesty. And though I will never give physical birth to children, I will be in labor many times with the new children You send into my life. But that's what woman's role is all about, isn't it? To be a life-bearer. And the life we bear is You, Jesus, to be carried into the world and given to all men. Praise Jesus!"

Heading north on I-75 back toward the convent, I kept Chesty much in my thoughts. I wondered if he were involved with Mimi, since Officer Cirillo was so certain she was a pusher. Who could get through to Chesty before he was really hooked? Who would he trust enough? Of course—Toby!

I zoomed past the Colerain exit and kept going to the St. Bernard exit. I hoped to catch Toby before he left Roger Bacon for home. As I approached the school I inched my way through traffic and clusters of students from Bacon and O. L. A. That was too slow for me, so I parked the car and walked and shoved and pushed toward Roger Bacon. Several of the guys from our prayer group greeted me. It was their consensus that Toby was still in the school building.

Whispering some quick prayers, I walked in the front door of Roger Bacon and there he was—ever-smiling Toby holding up a wall and talking with a classmate.

Toby is an expert in giving bone-crushing hugs. Every time I've been on the receiving end of one of Toby's hugs I've associated it with being embraced by God. If God were to hug me, that's how I imagine it—an all-encompassing, strong, warm embrace. For real, man!

"You look like you got something on your mind, Sister Gus. Shoot."

"I do, Toby. One of our soul brothers needs help and I think you'd be the one to get to him."

"Who you meaning?"

152

"Chesty."

Toby whistled low and long. "That doll get him into trouble?"

"I don't know, Toby. I haven't seen Chesty at the prayer meetings for a while but I didn't get concerned about it. His practice schedules are such crazy times I thought he couldn't make it."

"We're through with practice sessions, Sister Gus. It's almost the end of the school year."

"Right. So there must be other reasons why he hasn't been coming."

"You got any ideas about that?"

"I do after this morning, Toby. I was coming out of Isabella's Christian Book Store on Vine Street when this big fellow bumps into me and pushes me against a bar front. Not intentional, I know. He was blind on drugs. When I looked him in the face, I realized it was Chesty. He didn't recognize me."

Toby didn't register surprise but he did indicate concern. "He's been on the stuff before, Sister Gus. Then he knocked it off when he started to come to the prayer meetings. I have a hunch that doll Mimi might have gotten him back on it again."

"We can't accuse her without any proof, Toby."

"Hey, you always stick up for that dame?"

"I feel there's hope for Mimi. We can love her into change."

"Well, maybe—But for right now, we got to get to Chesty—with or without Mimi."

"I figured you'd be the one who could get through to him, Toby. He trusts you."

"Don't sweat it, Sister Gus. I'll cruise around among the guys and see what vibes I get about Chesty. But you keep up the praying, hear? I'm still such a baby in this deeper walk with the Lord that I get kinda—I

153

dunno. Hyper? Nervous? Chicken? Yeah, chicken. So I need your prayer power. I want to be bold in witnessing like St. Paul says. Especially to my soul brother, Chesty. With all my super intentions, sometimes I cringe. Well, Sister Gus, here I go!"

Toby waved as he walked toward a group of the guys who were lagging behind. "Thank You, Jesus, for Toby. Walk with him and help him get to Chesty."

Walking toward my car, I smiled at the sight before me. Kurt was draped over the front of my Dodge Dart like a mermaid carving on the prow of an ancient sailing vessel. Even when Kurt was immobile, he seemed to be in motion.

"Hey, Sister Gus," Kurt shouted. "Wouldn't we stop traffic if I stayed here on your car as you drove up Colerain Avenue? Out of sight, man. Out of sight."

"Hi, Kurt. Been up to your usual devilment?"

"The musical is over. I'm not playing devil any more. But he sure is playing in my life. Like for real, man."

"You didn't think he'd leave you off the hook just because you're finished playing that part, did you?"

"Gee, I know better than that. The other guys—you know like Sam and Bo and Cullen—they've told me plenty about how the devil really gets after brand new Christians like me. I figured it would be coming. But you're never quite ready. It's wierd."

Viewing Kurt perched on the hood of my Dodge Dart I could rightfully beam. The Lord's power was so evident in Kurt's life. If the devil had been giving him a tough time of it, I was sure Kurt was up to the battle.

"Sister Gus, that Jesus manages to blow my mind at least once a day! You know that chick I used to squire around. The redhead with the pug nose. Well, I discovered she was really into smoke, dope, acid. You name it. And last week, she *quit!* You know why? Because the

154

Lord got after another friend of ours to go to her house every Friday on her night off. She's been doing this for two months and nothing was happening. You know how that can get to you, Sister Gus."

I nodded my agreement. I'd been down the narrow way many times before. But with trust in the Lord even when it looks so hopeless, Jesus always comes through.

Kurt glowed as he continued in his yoga-like perch. "Well, Sister Gus, this friend of mine (Sylvia—you know Sylvia) kept going back to see the redheaded chick. Sylvia sat down and told J. C.—our Friend and Buddy —that she didn't see that her visits were doing any good. Nothing was changing. You know—nobody was being converted or quitting dope, etc.

"Jesus is so cool. He kept telling Sylvia not to worry about it. Just let Him take care of it. And out of the blue, the redheaded chick tells Sylvia she's quitting the stuff. Praise God, Sister Gus. That's another one for you to pray about so she'll stay on the right way. Jesus is so good to us and us dumb people keep doubting His love even when He keeps showing us over and over again. He does all this good stuff in His own sweet time and I guess I just get impatient. That's when the old devil moves in. Jesus is neat. Even if He is a little slow at times." Kurt chuckled as he had during the play.

In a most serious mood, Kurt asked, "Sister Gus, what have you heard about the new prayer group?"

"Which group is that, Kurt?"

"I heard that some of the kids had broken off from the big Friday night group and were starting their own."

"Was the big group too frightening for them?"

"Naw, numbers doesn't have anything to do with it. They were griping because they felt like you and Father Richard and Brother Dennis were taking over. Giving too many orders and that kind of thing."

155

"We haven't given anybody 'orders,' Kurt. We've given teaching and suggestions."

"Yeah, I know that, Sister Gus. I've heard you. But these jokers don't seem to know that."

"There has to be a core group for every prayer group, Kurt. The Lord works through the core group to teach and guide the others. A core group is meant to serve."

"I realize that. Understand, I don't have any gripes with the set-up. I'm telling you their beef."

"Our greatest strength as I see it is in community. *Together* we come before the Lord to praise Him and wait upon Him. There will always be those fragmented individuals who are discontent with every group. They continually shop around and never make any definite commitment. If this new group is the Lord's work, it will flourish. If it isn't, it will die. Just that simple."

Taking a quick look at his watch, Kurt jumped down from his perch. "Gotta run, Sister Gus. I have a part-time job at White Tower. Say, if you know any high-powered quickie prayers, better start sending them up for Jazz. He's on the skids."

"Lord, not another one?" I thought. "More labor pains!"

Aloud I said, "What's his problem? Too big a load with college plus a job?"

"He can handle that load, Sister Gus. What he can't handle these days is sex. Once you're started walking with the Lord, sex takes on a new dimension. So when you tomcat around—WHAM! Your conscience starts to rip you apart. Then you start thinking about scrapping this whole Jesus bit. And that's prime time for Satan."

"Glad you told me about Jazz, Kurt," I commented as we waved our good-byes.

More labor pains, indeed. With his artistic temperament, Jazz vacillated in many areas. It seemed to me

156

that he hadn't gotten deep enough into Jesus to ward off his present difficulty. He was reticent to take the plunge, "the leap of faith" as Father Richard termed it. Lord Jesus, we praise You for Jazz, for his fears and shortcomings, for his many gifts and talents. Help him use them to Your glory.

This was turning into an Alumni Day for prayer group kids. As I turned on the ignition, I noticed Rachel walking from O. L. A. toward me. Alabaster Rachel appeared mighty cloudy this afternoon.

Rachel waved but didn't speak. Something about her movements seemed out of rhythm. "Need a ride, Rachel?" I asked.

"I could use one. I had to stay after school and missed my ride home," Rachel replied without her usual enthusiasm.

Before I even had the car in gear, Rachel was pouring out her heart complete with tears. "Oh, Sister Gus, I'm so down. I haven't been to the prayer meetings for weeks because I felt like I was putting on a front. So empty inside. I haven't been praying at all. My heart's not in it. It's like I'm drained. I don't know what's wrong. Everything seems to be closing in on me. My Mom's been drunk for days. I flunked my exams. I don't have a date for the prom. I'm confused about so many things. I've never been so miserable and unhappy—" The rest trailed off into a fresh outburst of sobbing.

With her crying, Rachel hadn't noticed that I'd driven to our convent instead of to her home. When her body was quiet again, I said, "Rachel, let's go into the chapel for a while and just rest in the Lord."

Rachel was too upset to argue with the suggestion. She, a box of Kleenex and I entered the chapel and were engulfed with peace. I had such a strong awareness of the Lord's presence with us.

157

Softly I said, "Rachel, right now let's lift up your mother to Jesus and ask Him to bind her obsession with alcohol and remove it from her. We ask Him to give your mother His perfect peace and joy so that she may know this is her true liberation—Jesus' love for her."

"Sister Gus, I feel so ashamed. I didn't mean to blab all that stuff I told you in the car. You've got enough on your mind without listening to me."

"You know I want to listen to you, Rachel. Anytime. I've told you that before and I mean it. The Lord has asked you to carry a heavy burden with your parents divorced and your mother an alcoholic. We are meant to share each other's burdens."

Rachel seemed more peaceful as she dabbed at her eyes again. The stillness of the chapel was conducive to quiet reflection. The silence was broken periodically by Rachel uttering the name of Jesus. A most perfect prayer.

When Rachel was again erect and calm, I invited her to join the Sisters for supper but she declined. "Gee, thanks, Sister Gus. I'd like to stay with you all for supper. But I'd better get home. I don't know about Mom—"

"I understand, Rachel. I'll take you home now."

The drive was a short one. Rachel and her mother lived in an apartment. "Thanks for the ride, Sister Gus. And for everything," Rachel said rather tearfully as she hugged me and got out of the car.

"I'll come in with you, Rachel. In case you need any help."

Rachel's face was distorted with fear and shame. She was undoubtedly remembering the many nights she had come home from school or the prayer meetings and found her mother drunk. I felt I should go with Rachel because she herself was so unglued at the moment. And I held my ground.

No one answered the door bell. Rachel finally unearthed a key in the bottom of her handbag. There was one light burning in the living room which looked dim and untidy. An empty bottle of bourbon was on the coffee table and when my eyes were accustomed to the semi-darkness, I noticed a woman lying on the couch.

With bleary eyes, Rachel's mother looked up at me and said, "Hi ya, honey. You bring my kid home? Thanks."

Rachel made an attempt to introduce us but her voice wasn't very steady. I ached for Rachel. For her mother, too.

"Why don't you make us some coffee, Rachel? Your mother would like some, too."

"That's right, honey," her mother agreed, with her tongue getting in the way of each word.

First came the coffee. Then tomato soup heavily laced with milk. Rachel's mother became very sick and after we got her cleaned up, Rachel and I put her to bed. I have no idea if she was alert enough to know what was going on around her, but Rachel and I knelt at her bedside. With our hands resting on her body, Rachel and I prayed for a healing for her mother—a healing from the demon alcohol and all its ramifications. We praised the Lord for hearing our prayer and thanked Him for what He was already doing in this woman to bring about her healing. Her body relaxed in peaceful sleep as Rachel and I left her room.

"Rachel, you keep claiming her healing. Often. The Lord has heard our prayer and His power will work a miracle. We have only to trust Him and let it be for His glory."

Tears were streaming down Rachel's cheeks as she hugged me and I prepared to leave. I felt a wonderful peace about Rachel's mother. I knew the Lord had already begun a great work in her—and in her daughter, too. And I praised Him all the way back to the convent.

I found a note for me on the bulletin board asking me to return a call. The party, unnamed, had called several times since noon. I didn't recognize the number.

As I dialed, I was recounting the events of the day and wondering if Toby had found Chesty as yet when a young girl's voice answered the phone. It seemed familiar but I couldn't be sure.

"This is Sister Gus returning a call made from this number. Are you the party who called me?"

A weak "Yes" responded from the other end of the line. I still couldn't identify the caller. I waited for the party to make some further comment but there was only silence.

Every convent gets its share of crank phone calls. But since this party had called several times and asked for me by name, I felt I should proceed rather than hang up.

"May I help you?" I asked.

After another pause, the weak voice said in almost a whisper, "This is Mimi. I'm calling about Chesty—"

"Yes, Mimi. Go on, please—"

Haltingly, Mimi continued. "Chesty came to my apartment this afternoon, about one. He was already stoned but he wanted more. I don't have any stuff. I've really been trying to stay clean. But he wouldn't believe me. He started to push me around—"

There was another long pause, then Mimi continued.

"He got real nasty, Sister Gus. Not like Chesty at all. The guy with him convinced him they should go somewhere else—I'm worried about Chesty. He was nice to me before—nicer than any guy had ever been. I don't want him to get hooked and hit the bottom—"

"I know what you're saying, Mimi. I saw Chesty earlier today on Vine Street and he was high then. I've

160

talked with Toby about him and if anyone can get to Chesty right now, I'm sure it's Toby. We've put it all in the hands of the Lord in prayer and He hears us. If I learn anything more about Chesty, I'll call you. OK?"

For a moment, it sounded as though Mimi were crying. Sniffling, at least. In the same weak voice, she said, "OK."

On a hunch, I asked, "You all right, Mimi? Your voice is so weak. Maybe we've got a bad connection—"

"It's not the connection. I haven't felt very strong ever since I got home from the hospital."

"Do you eat regularly, Mimi? And get your rest?"

"Sometimes."

"You need to do it to build up your health, Mimi. It doesn't happen by magic. We've got to work at being healthy. The fringe benefits of good health—inside and out—are terrific."

"I'll try."

"Keep in touch, Mimi. Maybe we can sit down and have a good talk someday when you're up to it."

"Yeah— Take care of Chesty— I'm worried." The receiver clicked in my ear. I'm sure my mouth was still hanging open in awe and surprise after I hung up. If Mimi were as concerned for Chesty as her call indicated, that was a large plus in her favor. This might be a turning point in her life. I prayed that it would be. How like the Lord Jesus to bring good out of evil!

13. She Walks

There he was standing in the middle of the parking lot under a floppy-brimmed brown felt hat. Toby—round, warm, smiling Toby.

I parked my car and walked toward Toby grinning in response to his smile. "I figured I'd catch you if I waited out here in the parking lot. Something I wanted to tell you before you go into the prayer meeting, Sister Gus."

"Good news?" I queried.

"Man, you know a soul brother only gives good news to a soul sister. Right?"

"Right."

"So I wanted to tell you I brought a friend of ours to the prayer meeting tonight."

"Toby, I can't stand the suspense. Who?"

Like a mischievous pixie, he answered, "Chesty."

"For real?"

"For real, man. In the flesh. Right inside. A bit shaky. But here because he wants to be."

Now it was my turn to squeal and give Toby a rib-crushing hug. I praised God with every cell. "Toby, you're a veteran now."

"A veteran what?"

"A veteran witness. That's what. A real, live, experienced disciple. And you said you were chicken!"

"That's the straight scoop, Sister Gus. I was chicken.

Must have been your prayers that got me through it. Chesty, too."

Raindrops were plopping off the brim of Toby's felt hat but neither of us made a move toward the indoors. O.L.A. had gotten too small for our prayer meetings and the Sisters at Ursuline Academy had invited us to use their chapel on Friday nights.

Toby beamed as he spoke. "Sister Gus, I just never dreamed the Holy Spirit could teach me so much in these past few days since you told me about our soul brother, Chesty. So much about faith and about prayer. I never knew the joy of being on my knees and praying, really praying for a brother. Not just reciting a litany of 'give me' petitions—but hurting *for* my brother and hurting *with* him. Only prayer could have got me through that.

"After you left Roger Bacon the other day, I started checking around with the guys about Chesty. The rumblings were strictly bad news. He'd gone back with that bunch he used to hang around with before he started coming to the prayer meetings regularly. They're all on the stuff and soon Chesty was back on it, too. He's been missing school, got fired from his job, had a real bust with his dad. Loused up but good.

"I didn't know where to start. I went home to change clothes and while I was getting dressed, that banner you made me hit me between the eyes. Like, WOW, man, where you been? This is where it's at—'His banner over me is love.' I knelt down there in my room and claimed that love for me and Chesty. If my Mom would have walked in and seen me there on my knees, she would probably have called the man in the white coat!"

It's a woman's privilege to get dewy-eyed once in a while. I knew the wet stuff on my face was more than raindrops. To experience the growth in Toby from the first time I'd met him until this moment made my head

163

swim. The Lord's power was at work in him in a wonderful way. Praise Jesus!

"Sister Gus, that Jesus is something else. While I was kneeling there in my room, I just felt like I could reach out and touch Him. And it wasn't even a church or anything like that. Just little old me all by myself in my room. Jesus seemed to be telling me to cool it. You know —don't sweat it. He was with me, like a soul brother. That's it. Number One Soul Brother! Yeah! And it seemed so clear that I should get a move on. Find Chesty and let the Lord work through me to say the right things to him.

"I knew one of those dudes Chesty hangs out with is a student at U.C. and has an apartment on Calhoun Street. I called the chick he dates and she gave me the address. You been on Calhoun Street, Sister Gus? Weird, man. Weird."

I nodded my agreement. Calhoun Street had a personality of its own. I could visualize that ancient apartment in which Carla and Daisy lived. And the young people leaning against the buildings, many with glazed eyes and immobile faces.

"The Lord led me right to that apartment. I'd never have found it by myself. It's one of those off-the-alley entrances, up three flights and back a long hallway. I knocked several times before this dude answered the door. He looked like he was walking in his sleep. I asked to see Chesty and this cat starts to give me a rough time. I guess Chesty heard my voice because there he was all of a sudden, smiling at me and saying, 'Hey, man, let my soul brother in.' The guy couldn't argue with that so he motioned me inside.

"I don't mind telling you, Sister Gus, I was sweating bullets. I was scared. The place smelled strange and looked so hazy. Must have been four or five other guys

164

there all sort of out-of-it draped over the couch or chair or floor. Chesty whacked me on the back and we sat down at a table in the kitchenette.

"Sister Gus, if my life depended on it, I couldn't tell you what I said to Chesty." Toby's face was creased in a frown as though the mystery of it all still puzzled him greatly. He continued. "I know it was the Lord speaking through me. Jesus gave me the words to say, the words Chesty needed to hear. I forgot about being scared. My voice was calm and quiet like as though the Lord was even controlling the volume as well as content. Chesty was looking me right in the eyeballs. He was listening, man. Every so often I'd slip in a quick prayer to the Holy Spirit between sentences. 'Holy Spirit, keep giving me the right words,' and He did. Wow!

"Before I knew what was happening, Chesty had put on his jacket and grabbed my arm. He steered me out of the kitchenette and said, 'Let's split, man. I'm going with you, Toby.' Well, man, I wasn't going to give him any static about that. The other dudes were too stoned to care if we were coming or going so we just walked by them and out of that rat trap.

"Chesty came home with me. My folks weren't home from the movie yet so I got him some chow. He wolfed it down like he hadn't eaten in days. Never said a word. I told him he could sleep in my room until he got himself together. When he walked in my room, that banner hit him, too, and he sort of fell apart at the seams. I had visions of him going into withdrawal symptoms and the whole bit and I was about to call you, Sister Gus, to find out what I should do to bring him out of it when he quieted down. The Lord seemed to be telling me that we should praise Him and that was A-OK with me. Chesty nodded his head that he wanted to praise the Lord but no words would come. So I did the praying out loud while

Chesty praised the Lord in his heart. I know he was praying because that's the only way you get the peace that settled on him.

"In a short while he was sleeping like a baby. From then on, he can't stop praising the Lord. He kept asking me if I thought it would be all right for him to come tonight. When we got here, he had his answer. Sam and Cullen and Bo and Kurt and some of the other guys were all over Chesty before he even got out of the car. He couldn't doubt they were glad to see him back. You know, Sister Gus, that's what I figure heaven's going to be like—all our soul brothers waiting there to welcome us in. Ya-hoooooo!"

Toby and I were both more than damp from the rain. We walked toward the chapel greeting others along the way. I was so filled with joy I felt I would burst a blood vessel any moment. Brother Dennis was playing the opening song, one he had composed himself. I scanned the crowd and noted the new faces and the regulars. Up front beside Father Richard sat the bulk of Chesty. Praise Jesus!

The chapel at Ursuline Academy is very well suited to prayer. You can create various effects with the lights, too. Its stark simplicity appealed to me. And the unique tabernacle fitted into the wall behind multicolored slats intrigued me. Even so early in the prayer meeting, I felt a strong anointing of the Spirit on the group. For me this has always been one of the most adventuresome aspects of the charismatic movement. There is no predicting the flow, the trend, the theme of a prayer meeting. Each one is absolutely unique and unpredictable. The Holy Spirit will not be programmed or predicted or computed or confined. Alleluia!

I recognized Father Richard's voice praying, "Heavenly Father, we come together before You to praise You and thank You for this day, for the gift of life, for Your Son and Spirit. We are grateful for Your many gifts, for Your kind mercy which You show to us new each day. Fill us with the power of Your Spirit. Teach us to listen to You, to each other, to Your Word, to what the world is saying to us. Father, teach us to pray!"

Someone started to sing "Spirit of the Living God" and soon the very walls of the chapel were vibrating with the plea, "fall afresh on all." The Spirit was falling afresh if we would only open our hearts to receive Him. We were standing praising the Lord when I felt an arm around my waist. I looked next to me to find sweet Julie and I squeezed her so hard I'm sure it hurt. But I had to let her know how happy I was to have her with us. Sweet Julie was smiling through her tears and so was I.

During a quiet time, I heard Phyllis's voice reading Scripture from Philippians 4:4–8, words that seemed to envelop Chesty and sweet Julie and all of our kids.

I want you to be happy, always happy in the Lord; I repeat, what I want is your happiness. Let your tolerance be evident to everyone: the Lord is very near. There is no need to worry; but if there is anything you need, pray for it, asking God for it with prayer and thanksgiving, and that peace of God, which is so much greater than we can understand, will guard your hearts and your thoughts in Christ Jesus. Finally, brothers, fill your minds with everything that is true, everything that is noble, everything that is good and pure, everything that we love and honour, and everything that can be thought virtuous or worthy of praise.

Happy in the Lord—no need to worry—asking God for it with prayer and thanksgiving—fill your minds with

167

everything that is true—noble—good and pure—virtuous and worthy of praise. So much there to chew on. Where had the time gone? Father Richard was getting ready for Mass and Sam was lighting the candles. I sensed an aura of expectancy. The liturgies at our prayer meetings had always been meaningful and pertinent. The Spirit seemed to have a special anointing reserved for His minister at the altar. As Father Richard began, I was doubly convinced of the special anointing of the Spirit this night.

"We have not stepped out in faith and preached the seeming absurdity of the Word of God," Father Richard remarked. "As Isaiah tells us, this word of God when preached in faith does not return empty. You must want to be that rich soil that receives the Word of God. If there is no faith, it is because the Word has not been preached. We don't evangelize our people. We don't teach Christ's liberation. The Word of the Lord does not make sense to human minds. It only makes sense in the living of it. The Word of the Lord is a dangerous Word because it demands everything. Man doesn't like to hear it. Man stops up his ears.

"You must come to the point where you know that you need a Savior, a Lover. You have to come to that stage of littleness to know that you need Jesus. Jesus is saying, 'Turn around. There's a whole world you don't even know is there.'

"If you haven't taken the Word seriously, you don't know what you're missing. But you have to want it. Until you have created at the cost of pain, you do not have the resources to love. Love lays down its life. You give that person you love power over you. Love asks everything but we don't want to give everything so we run from it and kill it. You're nobody until Somebody loves you and that Somebody is Jesus. Once you're in the Spirit the Lord becomes so real to you. That's the gift of the Spirit.

It's heaven all the way to heaven! It's the Christian adventure, that Jesus joy that fills every moment, every event of your life."

I praised God for the gift of preaching he had given to Father Richard who speaks of the Good News like it is—simple, radical, challenging. Guaranteed to make you uncomfortable because you realize how your own hang-ups get in the way of the Good News.

As I was coming toward the back of the chapel after receiving Communion, I noticed Rachel sandwiched against the wall. I slithered down beside her and judged by her smile that the situation at home was improved. Rachel whispered in my ear, "Sister Gus, you'll never guess who came with me tonight—my Mom! I felt the Lord wanted me to ask her to come and I did. And she accepted the invitation. Would you believe, she hasn't had any booze since the night we prayed over her? Praise God!"

Looking at Rachel and sharing in her gladness I thought of the last words of Father Richard's homily "— that Jesus joy that fills every moment, every event of your life." Thank You, Jesus, for Your joy. Thank You for the healing You're working in Rachel's mother—and in Rachel, too.

In the closing prayer, Father Richard gathered all our petitions to present them to the Father. Then Father Richard said, "Expect everything from God. Ask everything from God. Open up your heart and allow the Lord to love you—Father, we praise You and thank You for hearing our prayer—the prayers we have spoken and those in our hearts. You know the needs of each one here. Just fill those needs, Father. Let it be to Your glory. We ask this in the all-powerful name of Your Son, Jesus, our brother and redeemer—"

The hushed atmosphere was shattered by the voice

of a young girl repeating, "I can walk—I can walk—I can walk—" Indeed she was walking right toward Father Richard and soon was embracing him and crying. I had never seen her at a prayer meeting before, and when she had come into the chapel earlier in the evening, I noticed she was being helped by several young people. The nurse in me diagnosed her condition as cerebral palsy and I wondered why she didn't have a wheelchair to improve her mobility. But now she was walking unassisted. Could it be—our first miracle?

There was a general movement of excitement as Brother Dennis started to play the recessional, "I Will Raise Him Up." If this were a miracle, the song was so appropriate. This young woman, slim and raven-haired, was indeed raised up into an upright walking position. Carrie and Toby were talking with Chesty and I asked if they knew our miracle girl. Carrie identified her as Megan—first time ever at our prayer meeting. Carrie commented further, "Megan is a great gal but I was surprised to see her here. Because of her condition, her mother never lets her go anywhere. Over-protective kind, you know. Did you see her walk, Sister Gus? It's a miracle for sure."

"Carrie, did Megan have much difficulty in walking?"

"Difficulty? Wow, I'll say. She's a C.P. and she couldn't control her gait. I'd heard they were getting her a special wheelchair. Doesn't seem like she'd have to have one now though. Isn't it super to think she was healed here at our prayer meeting?"

"That Jesus did it again," Toby interjected. "We didn't even ask for any special healing but He did it anyway just because He loves us so much."

Chesty appeared thoughtful as he commented, "This has been a week for healings. Right, Toby?"

"Right, man!"

"Seems that it happened when Father Richard mentioned the prayers in our hearts, the needs of each one that our heavenly Father knows and can fill. Remember he prayed, 'Let it be to Your glory' and this miracle truly is to His glory. I get inside out goose bumps just thinking about it again," I exclaimed.

"Wait until this gets around Cincinnati," Carrie chirped. "There will probably be a king-size inquisition to investigate."

"We can all testify. We saw it happen right here in front of our eyes," Toby added.

"I think the most static is going to come from Megan's parents."

"Why do you say that, Carrie?" I asked.

"I've been over to Megan's house and they just seem to want to keep her an invalid. They never want her to think for herself or make decisions 'because she's crippled.' This will blow their minds. They're not churchy people. You know what I mean, Sister Gus?"

"Yes, I do. Perhaps it would be good if the four of us agreed right now to lift up Megan and her parents in prayer and just keep claiming this healing for her. Agreed?"

"Agreed," they all chorused.

As the crowd thinned out and we were locking up, I managed to capture Father Richard's ear for a moment. Following the usual pattern after a prayer meeting, I'm sure at least a dozen or more young people had cornered him to share a problem, seek a solution, confide their troubles. And he paid the price for being so available and open to listening—a profound weariness. That weariness was evident in his face and movement.

"Praise the Lord, Richard. Do you think the Lord has blessed us with a healing in Megan?"

Father Richard heaved a deep sigh, the kind that starts at your toenails and then replied, "Gus, have you

171

ever felt the power of the Lord's presence so strongly as tonight? I mean all during the prayer meeting."

"It was extraordinary—extraordinarily wonderful! I have a feeling there were several healings here tonight—Megan's being the most outstanding because it was so dramatic."

"Who else was touched by the Lord?"

"Chesty, for one. He'd hit the bottom and the Lord pulled him back up again with the help of Toby. Rachel's mother. I see a real healing there. And a healing in Rachel, too. She's been torn apart by her parents' divorce and her mother's alcoholism."

"And countless others we'll never know about," Richard commented thoughtfully. "Praise Jesus for taking such good care of us."

"Did you get a chance to talk with Megan after the prayer meeting?"

"Only for a short time. She was still crying so hard it was difficult to understand what she was saying at times. But the kids who brought her to the prayer meeting supplied some of the details. As a nurse you probably realize she's had cerebral palsy. Gradually her muscle tone has deteriorated and her family is in the process of getting her a wheelchair.

"Our kids have been telling Megan about the prayer meeting for months but when she asked her parents, they wouldn't give her permission to come. I guess they got tired saying 'No' and tonight they gave their consent 'for this one time only.' So the kids lifted her in and out of the car and got her into the chapel."

"Her coming at all is a sort of miracle," I commented.

"Another way of the Lord showing us He'll get the kids here if we're willing and open to receive them," Richard agreed. "Megan said she was very interested in the prayer meeting because it was so different from what she had expected. She thought it would be rather formal with definite Scripture passages decided in advance and a prepared music program. That sort of thing. She appreciated the informality and spontaneity but couldn't believe these were Catholic kids. As she says it, 'They sounded so Protestant.' Well, we've heard that observation plenty of times before. Yes?"

"Amen!"

"Megan says she began to notice something different happening in herself during the liturgy—in the place where I said something about our having to reach a stage of littleness to know that we *need* Jesus. She didn't go forward to receive Communion because the chapel was so crowded and she was afraid she'd fall. But Sam, God bless him, noticed she wasn't moving and asked if she wanted to receive. She nodded affirmative and Sam came up to me and directed me back to where she was sitting. That's the first time I had seen her.

"A great peace filled Megan after she had received the Body and Blood of our Lord. She says she remembers my saying 'Expect everything from God. Ask everything from God.' She thought how wonderful it would be if she could walk like the other kids. Then all of a sudden, her legs felt as though they were on fire. A current seemed to be passing through her whole body. Then as though some force grabbed her by her clothing and stood her erect, she found herself standing unassisted and her legs were moving. She was walking. You know the rest, Gus."

It was so quiet now that all the kids were gone. Ours were the only two cars in the parking lot. The night was clear after the rain. I was shivering though the night breeze was balmy. The awesomeness of all Richard had said filled me with wonder at the mystery of love of God operative in our midst.

173

"Richard, we'd better put on the armor! The devil is really going to go after our kids to try to discredit what we've experienced tonight. And from what Carrie tells me, Megan is in for a rough time of it from her folks."

"The Lord's running this show, Gus. We'll continue to lift it all up to Him. I haven't seen all that many dramatic healings in my priestly ministry—probably because I didn't have enough faith to ask for them—but those I have seen always seem to be a prelude of something greater. What I'm saying is that the Lord heals them so that they may go on to some greater work for His glory. We can pray for His sustaining love for Megan so she can realize more and more how much He loves her."

"Richard, do you know what I'm reminded of when you said 'probably because I didn't have enough faith to ask'? I think of a story I heard about the man who died and went to heaven. St. Peter was giving him the grand tour and they came to an area covered with warehouses as far as you could see. The man asked St. Peter what was in all those numerous warehouses and St. Peter answered, 'Those warehouses are filled with all the blessings and graces God had for you—but you never asked.' We don't ask!"

"Let's praise the Lord for a minute before you drive off," Richard suggested.

There in the middle of the asphalt, east of the midnight, a prayer of praise and thanksgiving was raised to the Most High to thank Him for His trust in us to have worked such a great miracle in our midst and to praise and thank Him for all the miracles He worked which we would never learn about in this life. The night air was filled with praise for a loving Father so close to us that we felt His presence, so loving that we could not doubt His love, so real that we could reach out and touch Him in our life and in the life of our kids. Praise God!

174

I drove off toward Route 275 prayerfully flying high even though I was tied down to the mechanics of an ordinary automobile.

The news of our miracle girl spread rapidly through the prayer groups of Cincinnati, denominational and inter-denominational. In most instances, those participating praised and thanked the Lord for His mercy and kindness in working a miracle. And then there were the skeptics, the doubters who chalked it all up to emotions and hysteria. As the deluge of diversified opinions descended on us, I decided to do some investigating on my own.

On the next Wednesday afternoon, sunny and warm, I called Megan's home and asked if I might stop by to visit. A woman's voice answered, very precise and businesslike. She informed me that Megan had been upset but if I thought it necessary, I could stop by. Navigating isn't one of my talents but eventually when I stopped trying and let the Lord direct me, I found Megan's home. It was a comfortable middle-class dwelling in one of the more conservative sections of Cincinnati.

Megan's father answered the door and motioned me in. Her mother was all refined icicles. I felt as though I were walking into a giant deep-freeze until I met Megan. Her smile was like a neon sign and I just knew right off we would be great friends in the Lord.

After the usual pleasantries, tea and cookies, Megan and I were alone. Megan glistened with that fire and power that comes to those who have met the Lord and given themselves completely to Him. She walked without difficulty, erect and regal, like a queen.

"Sister Gus, I'm so glad to meet you. The kids have told me about you but I never thought I'd really meet you."

"Well, Megan, the Lord arranged our meeting and it's real. I wanted to meet you after the prayer meeting last

175

Friday night but there were so many people milling about, I couldn't get to you. Do you realize you're very special?"

"Special?"

"Yes, Megan, special in the eyes of the Lord and in our eyes. We had never seen you before but we know you have to be special for the Lord to touch you with a healing. And we know He must have some very specific plans for you to have worked a healing. That's not an everyday occurrence, you know!"

In a most disconsolate voice, Megan replied, "Don't get so excited, Sister Gus. No one believes me. No one believes I've been healed. Even my own mother says it's hysteria."

The tears were flowing and it seemed as though they had been pent up for days.

Between sobs, Megan sputtered, "My folks want to have me commited to a mental institution. They say I'm psycho. You're a nurse, Sister Gus. Do you think I'm psycho?"

I reached out to Megan in body and spirit. "Megan, you know enough about the Gospel to realize how Jesus was rejected by His own. I don't have to spell that out for you. If Jesus met that kind of mistrust, we have to know we will, too. Praise and thank Him, Megan, that He trusts you enough to place you right in the middle of such rejection so soon in your new Christian life."

"But what can I do now, Sister Gus?" Megan pleaded.

"For right now, Megan, rest in the Lord. Hang loose! He loves you. He's proven that. And He is with you. Let Him really take over your life. Trust Him to change hearts—the hearts of your parents and family who label your healing hysteria. This is going to be the greatest adventure of your life, Megan. Believe that!"

A calm settled on Megan. The tears had stopped and she was smiling as she commented, "I'll never forget last

Friday night, Sister Gus. Never. It's one night of my life that I will share with others over and over. I know the Lord will take care of all these other difficulties because I'm not able to do it. I've given the total thing to Jesus. I respect my parents and I love them. Maybe I can do like you say, Sister Gus—love them into change. I'm trying."

"Megan, believe that your folks really want the best for you. Without any background or personal experience in this sort of thing, a real miracle, you must understand that they would question and doubt what we call a miracle. So many, many feel that miracles stopped with Jesus' death on the cross. That's not true. We know that. But not everybody believes that there are plenty of miracles happening every day of the world because someone somewhere has faith that Jesus hears and honors our prayer."

Megan twisted her handkerchief but she did seem to be more at peace. There was a slight tremor in her hands but she seemed serene compared to most C.P. sufferers.

I felt urged to pray with Megan so I suggested it and she agreed. Claiming the scripture that says "where two or three are gathered in my name, there am I in the midst of you," I began our prayer.

"Jesus, we praise You and thank You for what You are doing in our lives. We again state our commitment to You, Jesus. Give us Your Scripture teaching so that we may learn Your will. Teach us in Your Word. Praise You, Jesus."

I opened my Bible to Isaiah 10:24–25 which spoke to us in this moment of trial. "Do not be afraid . . . A little longer, a very little, and fury will come to an end . . ." Praise Jesus! A little longer—

"Sister Gus, that's beautiful," Megan sighed. "That really gives me courage. But I'm concerned because my mother says I can't go back to another prayer meeting. Sister Gus, I *need* the kids."

"I know you do, Megan. The Lord knows it, too. Trust Him. He can change your mother's heart. And if you can't get to the prayer meetings, we'll come to you. OK?"

Megan was too moved to speak. No wonder the Lord had chosen her for His own. Such a lovely, prayerful soul. So full of hope and zeal. A chosen instrument.

As I left her home, I continued praising and thanking the Lord for Megan, for her mother, the great stone face; for her father, impassive and brooding. I felt their eyes boring through me but I rejoiced to know the power of the Lord was so strong in this household in Megan.

Megan's father accompanied me to the front door. He closed it behind us as he stared hard at me. His facial expression mirrored the hostility churning inside him.

"Lady," he barked, "I don't know how you're connected with this Friday night bunch but I'm thinking of getting the law after you. That's a pretty lousy trick you pulled to get Megan and those other kids all stirred up. It's hysteria. That's what it is—hysteria!"

His voice increased in volume with each sentence. There's no point in arguing with a mule. You've got to love them where they're at. And I was trying to do just that.

"We've had Megan to the best doctors in Cincinnati," he continued. "Each one of them has told us there was no hope of improvement. They told us she wouldn't walk, so we're getting her a wheelchair. They've told us to be grateful her brain damage isn't greater than it is. I believe those doctors. But I don't believe what I'm seeing and hearing in Megan since Friday. It's hysteria. And if she doesn't come to her senses soon, we'll have her commited to Longview. Do you understand? We'll have her commited!"

178

His fury was seething. Neighbors across the street were looking in our direction. I couldn't understand myself. Ordinarily my Yugoslav temper would have matched his but I felt very peaceful as I stated matter-of-factly, "I've been a nurse for twenty-five years. What I saw on Friday night and what I see today in Megan is not hysteria. It is a miracle, pure and simple. A miracle of God Who loves Megan very much. And He loves you, too."

With that I walked off the porch and down the street to my car. "That one is going to need some tall praying," I thought as I started the car. How can we be so blind not to accept God's miracles? Some children playing near the stop sign on the corner gave me a big wave and "Hi, Sister." Another one of God's miracles—children playing and romping out in God's sunshine. Glorious! Praise You, Lord, for the infinite number of miracles all around us that we take so for granted. Praise You for a new day, for the gift of life, for Your sunshine, for Your Son and Spirit. Be with Megan in a special way in these days ahead. Strengthen her faith as You strengthen her legs and arms. We claim this miracle of healing for her in the all-powerful name of Jesus, our brother and redeemer.

At the next stop light I took a minute to drink in the beauty of a rosebush near the sidewalk. The blooms were such a delicate pink, like Megan's complexion. "It will be interesting to see what You have planned for this young lady, Lord," I thought. She reflects Your beauty as much as that lovely rosebush I just passed. Praise You, Jesus!"

14. The Citadel

Since our meeting with Archbishop Leibold in February, Father Richard had checked out several proposed sites for the future TEC Lodge. In the archdiocese there were schools, convents, churches not in use. Each time we built up our hopes they were dashed again by the realization that the newest suggested site was inadequate for space, required too many repairs, in an undesirable section of the city—

Throughout the months of waiting, we continued to receive the same Scripture teachings indicating we had only to trust in the Lord. He would provide the place. Sometimes when we'd be together with some of the kids we'd have a brainstorming session and throw out a wild assortment of facilities we thought the new TEC Lodge should encompass. Plenty of acreage on which to roam—a lake or at least a brook—trees, lots of trees—hermitage—swimming pool—flowers, lots of flowers—prayer room—space for Father Richard and the Brothers working with him to live-in—plenty of kitchen space for Granny—music room—

When any of us from the prayer group met, the initial question was always the same. "Any news of another TEC Lodge yet?" That question popped up in the most unexpected places. One May day I had gone to Sears to pick up a parcel and I ran into Phyllis. She had a summer job at Sears and her bubbly personality was right at home in the toy department.

"Hi, Sister Gus," she squealed. "Any news of a TEC Lodge as yet?"

"No, Phyllis," I said for the umpteenth time that month. "None yet. But it will come."

"I dunno. I'd like to think the Archbishop is going to come through like he said, but he's so busy. And summer is moving right along. No time to waste."

Phyllis was truly representative of the NOW generation. She wanted instant everything! But it was good to see her so radiant after some of the dark moments we had shared several months ago. In March she had broken her leg while riding with a friend on his Suzuki. Phyllis was hospitalized for several weeks but was up and about now with no apparent difficulty.

"You all glued together now?"

Phyllis lifted her mended leg. "You bet. I just told Jesus I didn't intend to spend weeks in bed and out of the action and He'd better get busy and heal me. So He did! I'm good as new."

"Have you given up riding the Suzuki?"

"Sister Gus, you crazy or something? I wouldn't give up all those thrills just because of one lousy broken leg. That was a freak accident. Won't happen again."

I admired her optimism but I wasn't all that sure about the safety record of motor bikes.

"Besides I needed that hospitalization," Phyllis continued. "The Lord arranged it so I could get my head together. I've been in and out of the desert and I've learned a lot. When I first went to the hospital, I was on the mountain top. Then when I began to lose that top-of-the-mountain excitement, I pushed the panic button. I realize now that the Spirit was so strong in the beginning because I was in such need. Now that the crisis is over I

181

don't need that constantly penetrating kind of radiance to maintain my sanity and self.

"You know one thing I've discovered, Sister Gus? You can never sit back on your rusty-dusty and think, 'I've got it made.' Jesus just doesn't stand for that kind of lethargy without planting a bombshell somewhere in your life. Do you read me?"

"I do, Phyllis. After that black Ash Wednesday we shared, the Lord took you to the mountain top. But none of us can ever stay on the mountain top all the time or we'd never grow. Jesus brings us down low, sometimes very low so we can better realize that without Him, we're nothing."

Phyllis was putting some Raggedy-Ann dolls on the shelf and her impish expression matched that of the dolls. She seemed charged with electricity when she spoke.

"Sometimes I can't believe I'm me. You know, Sister Gus, I mean after that Ash Wednesday session, I just said, 'Jesus, change me where and how I need to be changed.' And although I can't put my finger on specific areas where I've changed, I know I'm different. It's curious to me that I can accept things now that before were unacceptable. This has meant some painful changes. It's strange, Sister Gus, to know, really know, with a cold, harsh knowledge that you were crummy yet refused to do anything about it. But Jesus strengthened me when I needed it most. Anyway, who says being a Christian is easy?"

How I welcomed Phyllis's smile and exuberance. I'd wager the toy department sales had gone up since she's on their staff. Her bubbly joy and enthusiasm were contagious.

"I've got to run, Phyllis, and I know you're busy here with your job. It's been such a joy talking with you and seeing you smile. Keep spreading that Jesus joy. Hear?"

"Yeah, Sister Gus. I hear you." Phyllis included a

182

Raggedy-Ann doll in our good-bye hug. We made quite a trio.

On the drive back to the convent, I decided to take a quick detour through Mount Airy Forest to absorb some of nature's beauty there. In the heart of the forest, I parked the car and got out to walk. Every city and town should have a forest—a haven of trees and streams and birds and crawling things where one can unwind and be refreshed.

Suddenly it seemed to be autumn again—the past autumn—when Bart and I had walked this same path dodging a Frisbee disc. Multiple changes had transpired in Bart's life and mine since that autumn day. His dire warnings about my involvement in youth ministry hadn't materialized. Praise God! The Lord had blessed our efforts with youth beyond our wildest dreams. And the peace experienced each day as I lifted Father Richard and those young people up to the Lord convinced me that we had only just begun. The Lord had even more lavish gifts in store for us!

Have you ever closed your eyes and been able to see faces with your mind's eye? As I did it sitting there on a huge boulder in Mount Airy Forest, I saw many faces —faces of those I dearly love. Priscilla, with the tears streaming down, squealing "Jesus is so real." And Chrissie coming to my hospital room to say "Thank you." Cullen, Bo and Sam—that invincible triad—such a source of strength to all of us. Father Richard, Brother Dennis, Brother Mark—men of God, men of prayer, rich in God's gifts. Sara Kate and Molly, Rachel and Sylvia—how they had grown in the Lord. Toby and Chesty, Mitch and Kurt—fighting some rough battles to stay afloat; but they were winning. The Lord was on their side!

Sweet Julie—broken physically and emotionally—had

183

been healed by the body ministry. They had loved her back into wholeness. To me, she was lovelier than ever with the deep-down kind of loveliness that comes with suffering and pain that is borne with joy and peace. On the opposite side of the spectrum was Mimi. How could we reach her for the Lord?

A battered Chevy charged past me on my rocky perch, stopped suddenly, and backed up. Jazz jumped out of the car and greeted me.

"Hey, Sister Gus. For a minute as I drove by I thought you were the latest statuary addition to Mount Airy Forest. You were so still there on top of your mountain of rock. Hope I'm not interrupting anything."

"Hi, Jazz. It's good to see you. Are your classes out for the day?"

"Yeah, classes are finished. Thought I'd cruise around a while and blow the cobwebs out of my brain. Say, are you coming to graduation tonight at XU? Your buddy, Archbishop Leibold, will be there."

"Sorry I'm going to have to miss it. I'll depend on you to tell me all about it."

"Will do."

"Things going any better for you, Jazz?"

Jazz was rolling a daisy in his palm and seemed engrossed in it for a time before he answered. "If you mean me and school, I'm holding my own in classes. If you're referring to me and dames, it's a hard battle for me. What I think you mean, though, is between me and Jesus, and man that is strictly *wow*. I can't understand why I fought Him off for so long. How do you suppose Jesus puts up with the likes of me, Sister Gus?"

"He puts up with the likes of each one of us because He loves us. It's so simple—His love that keeps picking us up each time we blow it."

184

"I think I've been driving my religion prof ape with some of my questions lately."

"Don't be too hard on your professor. He probably welcomes your interest. Religion class is often a mighty dry affair."

"Dry? Desperately dry, man! I keep thinking what a powerhouse religion classes could be if there were some genuine enthusiasm and conviction. Not so much all this intellectual stuff. More of the heart and personal application. Know what I mean?"

"I do know. But I also realize you need that intellectual background, too. Jazz, you have the potential to be a real leader in our prayer community because you've battled so many personal hang-ups to get where you are with the Lord. When you're a leader, you're also a teacher. Being a teacher doesn't come by magic. You need background in theology and Scripture—good, solid background— which you're getting at XU."

"I read you, Sister Gus. I'm just naturally impatient. Not that I'm copping out, understand, but I'm thinking of fading out of the collegiate scene—at least as a full-time student. I'm shopping around for a job that I can handle with night school. But I'm still praying about that step. Pray with me?"

"You know I do, Jazz. The Lord will show you the way He wants you to go. Claim it."

"Right on. I've got to split and get my gear ready for tonight. See you at the prayer meeting Friday."

Jazz revved up his ancient chariot and drove off in a burst of pebbles and dust. He had so much talent—musically, artistically, intellectually. Lord, help him use these gifts for Your glory!

A Park Patrol cruiser drove by and I thought again of the night Jazz and I had invited the policeman into the prayer meeting at the pink house on Brookside. If we only knew where our new location for the TEC Lodge was to be! Perhaps when the flurry of commencements and confirmation ceremonies was over, the Archbishop might have time to consider our request. Soon, Lord. Let it be soon!

Thunder and lightning were heralding a storm as I drove the short distance from the Forest to our Motherhouse on Colerain Avenue. I said a little prayer that the storm might be over before the commencement exercises at XU were scheduled to begin.

Several errands kept me out until later that evening. As I entered the convent, my sisters greeted me with the news that Archbishop Leibold had been stricken during the commencement exercises at XU. He had been rushed to Good Sam Hospital: condition, critical.

For some reason, I felt as though the bottom had been knocked out of me. He was young for an Archbishop—only fifty-seven. I found myself thinking the same thoughts I had when Cardinal Meyer was dying with cancer of the brain in Chicago some years before. Why, Lord? Why? He has so much to offer the Church. We need him.

Who can fathom the ways of the Lord? I'm sure there were many all over the Archdiocese of Cincinnati who devoted a large part of that night to prayer for our Shepherd. At 2:30 P.M. the next day, June 1, 1973, our heavenly Father called Paul Francis Leibold home to Himself. Our Archbishop was dead.

I kept seeing his face before me—weary and ashen—as I had seen him in February. I remembered, too, the card I had sent him on May 18 for his ordination anniversary. On it I had penned one of my nurse-notes about "taking it easy." Now at last he was at rest in the New Jerusalem. And I found myself saying (as though he were with me in our chapel), "Paul Francis Leibold, I know

186

you're going to get us that new TEC Lodge. Soon." I asked the Lord for a Scripture teaching and picked up the Bible in the pew where I was kneeling. I opened it, upside down, and when I righted the page, I actually cried out as I read—that same memorable Scripture reading, confirmed so many times before and now again—from 1 Chronicles 28:20-21.

"Be strong, stand firm; be fearless, be dauntless and set to work, because Yahweh God, my God is with you. He will not fail you or forsake you before you have finished all the work to be done for the house of Yahweh. Here are the orders of priests and Levites for all the duties of the house of God; every willing man of any aptitude will help you in all this work; the officials and all the people are entirely at your command."

All manner of tribute was paid our Archbishop. There was an air of sorrow yet great peace to have known such a man of God in our midst as shepherd and servant. Media coverage was extensive. Church dignitaries from all over the land came to pay their respects together with our Jewish brothers.

I was at prayer during the funeral. Later when I was called to the phone, I was surprised to hear Father Richard's voice.

"Gus, you were right!" he said breathlessly.

"About what?"

"The Archbishop getting us a place."

"What do you mean?"

"I just got back from the Archbishop's funeral at the cathedral. As I walked into the monastery, Brother Mark told me I had a phone call. It was the president of the Board of Directors for the Crosley Estate."

"THE Top Brass?"

"Himself, Gus," Richard's voice conveyed his excitement. "And he told me the Crosley Estate is ours to use for the new TEC Lodge. Can you believe that?"

All I could do was whisper, "Praise Jesus," over and over. More than we ever dreamed. More than we ever asked. The Lord is never outdone in generosity. "Praise Jesus."

"When can we look it over, Richard?"

"Right now. Imagine. Now! And I can't think of a better way for us to end this day of Archbishop Leibold's funeral than to start making our plans for the TEC Lodge. Can you get away for a while?"

"Oh, yes! I'll meet you at the estate in half an hour."

"Great! That will give me time to hunt down the security guard and get the key from him. See you there."

I hung up the receiver mechanically and found I couldn't move. The news of a TEC Lodge available now on the same day as Archbishop Leibold's funeral was not coincidence to me. It was another awesome example of Jesus' loving care for us and our youth ministry, of a promise made and kept by a man deeply concerned with our youth—Paul Francis Leibold.

As I drove up Colerain Avenue toward Kipling, I praised the Lord in song and prayer. I felt as though I were flying but the periodic stop lights brought me to the reality I was driving. I turned into the circular drive at 2366 Kipling Avenue and as my eyes took in the expanse of the mansion, the grounds, lake, greenhouse, swimming pool, I wondered how many others had driven up to this massive front door. Yet of all those who had come to this impressive estate in the past, I had a distinct feeling that the best was yet to be.

Father Richard greeted me as the security guard drove